On the Beat 2

Student's Book

Catherine McBeth
Michele Crawford
Silvia Carolina Tiberio
Ron Martinez
Viviane Kirmeliene

On the Beat 2

Contents

UNIT	VOCABULARY	GRAMMAR	FUNCTIONS
It's my life! pp. 8–11	• School subjects • Dates • Home • Routines • Clothes	• *Be* • Possessive adjectives • Possessive *'s*	• Saying dates • Describing a room • Describing our routine • Identifying clothes • Talking about possession
UNIT 1 **What do you like?** pp. 12–23	• Free-time activities • Skills and abilities	• Simple present and present progressive • *love, hate, (don't) like, don't mind, enjoy + -ing*	• Talking about weekend activities • Contrasting routines with actions happening now • Describing skills and abilities • Expressing likes and dislikes
UNIT 2 **Music and TV** pp. 24–35	• Music • TV programs	• Simple past – regular and irregular verbs (1): affirmative and negative • *Be* – simple past: affirmative and negative	• Asking and answering about music, musicians, and bands • Talking about past events • Describing and giving our opinion on TV programs
UNIT 3 **Fact or fiction?** pp. 38–49	• Types of books • Verbs to talk about people's lives in the past	• *Be* – simple past: questions • Simple past – regular and irregular verbs (2): questions	• Giving our opinion on books • Asking and answering about past events • Talking about famous people's lives in the past
UNIT 4 **Life on Earth** pp. 50–61	• Geographical features • Environmental issues	• Adjectives: comparative and superlative forms • *a / an, some, any, not much / many, a lot of, How much / many...?*	• Describing natural wonders • Comparing places • Talking about environmental issues • Asking and answering about quantity
UNIT 5 **Special days** pp. 64–75	• Celebrations • Adverbs of manner	• *Going to*: affirmative, negative, and questions • Object pronouns • Present progressive for arrangements	• Describing celebrations and special days • Expressing intention • Describing the way we do things • Talking about arrangements
UNIT 6 **Take care** pp. 76–87	• Physical and mental health • Health problems and first aid	• *Should*: affirmative, negative, and questions • The infinitive of purpose	• Talking about physical and mental health • Asking for and giving advice • Talking about health problems and first aid • Expressing purpose

Workbook pp. 93–117

Consolidation (Units 1–3) & Project (a timeline) Ⓐ pp. 118 & 119

Consolidation (Units 4–6) & Project (a general knowledge quiz) Ⓑ pp. 120 & 121

creative corner pp. 122–130

READING & LISTENING	BUILD YOUR SKILLS	EXTRA READING, PROGRESS CHECK & WORKBOOK
	• **Listening & Speaking:** Getting to know people, p. 9	
• **Reading:** Posts on a teens website, p. 14 • **Listening:** A TV talent show, p. 17 • **Reading:** A magazine interview, p. 18	• **Reading & Listening:** An ad, p. 20 • **Listening & Speaking:** Asking for personal information, p. 21 • **Writing:** A personal profile, p. 22 Write it right! Giving reasons	**The Beat** p. 23 MAGAZINE • **Progress Check** p. 36 • **Workbook** pp. 94–97
• **Reading:** A magazine article, p. 26 • **Listening:** What was on?, p. 29 • **Reading:** TV programs reviews, p. 30	• **Reading & Listening:** A bulletin board, p. 32 • **Listening & Speaking:** Talking about likes and dislikes, p. 33 • **Writing:** A short biography, p. 34 Write it right! Past time expressions	**The Beat** p. 35 MAGAZINE • **Progress Check** p. 37 • **Workbook** pp. 98–101
• **Reading:** An online message board, p. 40 • **Listening:** Famous people in modern history, p. 43 • **Reading:** A magazine article, p. 44	• **Reading & Listening:** A festival web page, p. 46 • **Listening & Speaking:** Talking about past events, p. 47 • **Writing:** A review, p. 48 Write it right! Linkers	**The Beat** p. 49 MAGAZINE • **Progress Check** p. 62 • **Workbook** pp. 102–105
• **Reading:** A web article, p. 52 • **Listening:** Endangered animals, p. 55 • **Reading:** An online travel guide, p. 56	• **Reading & Listening:** An NGO leaflet, p. 58 • **Listening & Speaking:** Expressing preferences, p. 59 • **Writing:** A travel guide article, p. 60 Write it right! Order of adjectives	**The Beat** p. 61 MAGAZINE • **Progress Check** p. 63 • **Workbook** pp. 106–109
• **Reading:** Blog entries, p. 66 • **Listening:** Resolutions, p. 69 • **Reading:** Posts on a travel website, p. 70	• **Reading & Listening:** A festival leaflet, p. 72 • **Listening & Speaking:** Making arrangements, p. 73 • **Writing:** An invitation, p. 74 Write it right! Prepositions of time and place	**The Beat** p. 75 MAGAZINE • **Progress Check** p. 88 • **Workbook** pp. 110–113
• **Reading:** An information leaflet, p. 78 • **Listening:** Helpline, p. 81 • **Reading:** A magazine article, p. 82	• **Reading & Listening:** An online ad, p. 84 • **Listening & Speaking:** Talking about health, p. 85 • **Writing:** Emails, p. 86 Write it right! Asking for and giving advice	**The Beat** p. 87 MAGAZINE • **Progress Check** p. 90 • **Workbook** pp. 114–117

Speaking activities: Student A / B pp. 131 & 132

Irregular verbs p. 133

Audio transcripts pp. 134–136

Learning bank pp. 137–139

Walkthrough

Vocabulary easily and clearly presented at word (*chair, desk*) or phrase level (*go for a run, have breakfast*), as appropriate, through pictures / photos and within a context.

Quick and helpful information on **learning strategies** help maximize learning. Each strategy can be used as appropriate throughout the course.

Personalized Learning opportunities also create a deeper learning experience for students.

Texts of different formats will reinforce the vocabulary taught in the previous section, expose new grammar, and develop comprehension skills.

Skills strategies clearly signposted help prepare for the activity by showing which skill is most required to do it.

4

Clear examples of the target **grammar** taken from the text read in the previous section are explored in this section. **Use** and **form** of the language topic are inferred in context.

The second **vocabulary** section presents the second lexical set in the unit.

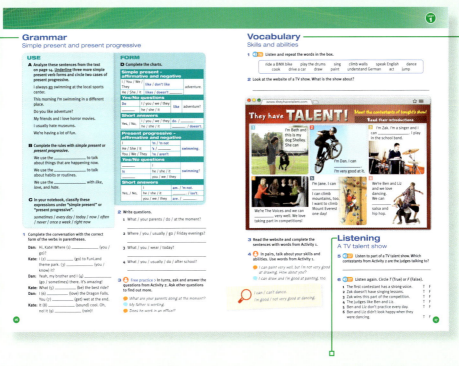

Engaging **listening** texts contain examples of the target vocabulary. They provide an opportunity to hear the new language in context.

The second **reading** section presents a new text followed by a pre- and post-reading activities.

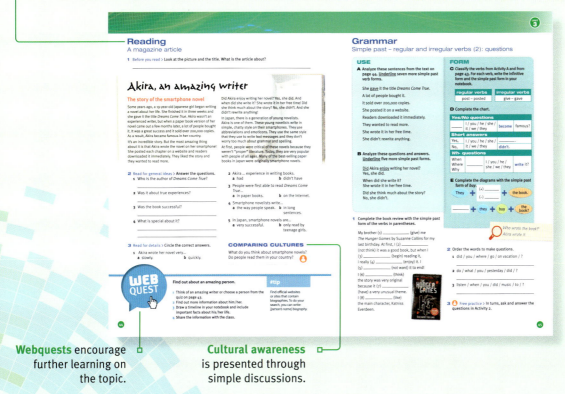

Webquests encourage further learning on the topic.

Cultural awareness is presented through simple discussions.

5

This section provides an opportunity to reinforce some of the language taught in the unit and practise three of the basic skills – reading, listening, and speaking.

Functional and natural language is presented through **audio stories**.

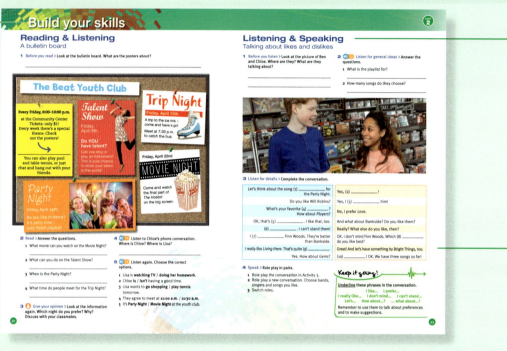

Conversational strategies help develop **oral fluency**.

A variety of formats are required to exercise **writing skills** with a communicative purpose. A model is always provided.

The Beat Magazine brings fun texts to read for pleasure and develop receptive skills. It also provides an opportunity to review the language learned in the unit.

Writing tasks are easily structured in a framework that help students develop their writing fluency.

6

Language consolidation every two units can be used in class or as extra homework.

The **Workbook** offers extra practice of the target language, which can be done for self-study, homework, or extra classroom practice.

Additional Resources

The **creative corner** includes adapted literary texts to promote further reading and to help pave the road to a more complex literary appreciation.

A useful self-study reference of all the language presented in each unit.

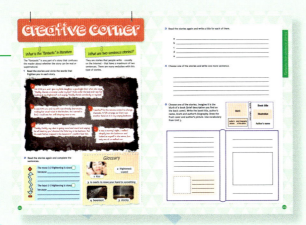

It's my life!

Vocabulary
School subjects

1 These are Lucy and Chris. What are their favorite subjects? What is Chris's favorite weekday?

_____

_____

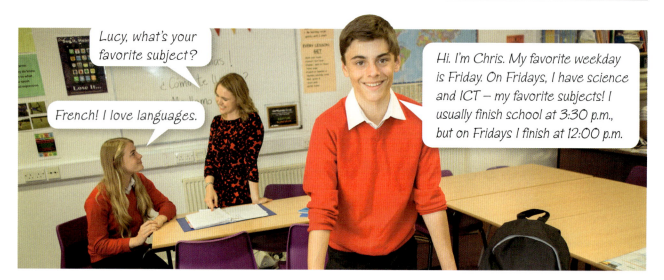

"Lucy, what's your favorite subject?"

"French! I love languages."

"Hi. I'm Chris. My favorite weekday is Friday. On Fridays, I have science and ICT – my favorite subjects! I usually finish school at 3:30 p.m., but on Fridays I finish at 12:00 p.m."

2 🔊 02 Look at the pictures and complete the school subjects. Then listen, check, and repeat.

1 __ __ __ h
2 __ r __
3 __ __ st __ __ __
4 __ __ T
5 d __ __ __ a
6 __ u __ i __
7 __ __ i __ __ e
8 g __ __ __ r __ __ __ __

3 Answer the questions.

1 What's your favorite weekday?

_____

2 What subjects do you have on that day?

_____

Dates

4 🔊 03 Say the dates. Then listen and check.

1 09/16/1996
2 02/28/2000
3 05/01/2011
4 01/03/2015

> 🔍 We write: *1991 / 2008*
> We say: *nineteen ninety-one / two thousand and eight*

5 In turns, say the dates of these special days.

1 Christmas Day
2 Flag Day
3 Independence Day
4 New Year's Day
5 Your birthday

🟡 *Christmas Day is on December 25th.*
🔵 *Flag Day is on…*

Listening & Speaking
Getting to know people

1 Before you listen > Look at the picture. Who are they? Where are they?

_____

_____

_____

2 🔊 **04 Listen for general ideas >** Answer the questions.

1 Are Lucy and Chris in the same year?

_____

2 Do they live near each other?

_____

3 🔊 **04 Listen for details >** Complete the conversation.

So, what's your (1) _____ ?	My name's Lucy. What about you?
I'm Chris.	Nice to (2) _____ you, Chris.
	What (3) _____ are you in?
I'm in 8th grade.	Me too! I'm in (4) _____ class.
Cool. Where do you (5) _____ ?	On Ash Road.
Oh, I live (6) _____ there.	OK, let's go!
Let's (7) _____ home together!	

4 Speak > Role play in pairs.

1 Role play the conversation in Activity 3.
2 Role play a new conversation. Use your own information.
3 Switch roles.

Keep it going!

Underline these questions in the conversation.

What's your name?   What about you?
What grade are you in?   Where do you live?

Use them when you meet people to get to know them. Use *Me too!* to say that something is also true for you.

Grammar
Be

1 Look at the chart and review.

Affirmative		
I	am	15 years old.
You / We / They	are	Chinese.
He / She / It	is	from Spain.
Negative		
I	am not	from Italy.
You / We / They	are not	in New York.
He / She / It	is not	my best friend.

2 In your notebook, rewrite the sentences in the chart using the short forms of *be*.

3 Circle *T* (True) or *F* (False). Then correct the false sentences in your notebook. Use short forms of *be*.

1 Great Britain is an island. T F
2 Yoko and Hans are English names. T F
3 New York is the capital of the United States. T F
4 British people's favorite drink is tea. T F
5 The Sydney Opera House is in Canada. T F

4 Look at the chart and review.

Yes/No questions		
Am	I	a teenager?
Are	you / we / they	friends?
Is	he / she	your teacher?
Short answers		
Yes,	I	am.
	you / we / they	are.
	he / she	is.
No,	I	'm not.
	you / we / they	aren't.
	he / she	isn't.

5 Answer about you. Use short answers.

1 Is this your first English lesson?
_____

2 Are your friends in your English class?
_____

3 Are you on page 15 of this book?
_____

4 Are you in the 1st grade of middle school?
_____

Vocabulary
Home

6 Look at the picture. What room is it? Write words for furniture.

7 Write a paragraph describing the room in Activity 6 in your notebook. Use *there is, there are, there isn't* and *there aren't*, and adjectives from the box.

> modern   old   tidy   clean   dirty
> nice   expensive

Routines

8 Write the activities from the box in the order you do them. Write the times. Then describe your daily routine to a classmate.

> go to bed   have breakfast   go to school
> take a shower   do my homework
> come back home   have lunch

My routine

Time	Activity

10

Vocabulary
Clothes

1 Match the pictures to the texts on the right.

Lucy

Chris

Nina

OUR FAVORITE CLOTHES

1 My favorite clothes are my **jeans**! I wear them with a **T-shirt** in the summer and with a **sweater** in the winter. I always wear **jeans**.
Who am I? ☐

2 I love my new **jacket**. It looks great with my **scarf** and my brown **boots**!
Who am I? ☐

3 This is my favorite **dress**. It looks nice with these **sandals**. I sometimes wear a **jacket** with it, if it's cold.
Who am I? ☐

2 Write other words for clothes.

skirt,...

Possessive 's

5 Analyze these sentences.

1 The dog**'s** coat is red.
's = possession

2 The boys**'** T-shirts are big.
s' = possession

3 Jane**'s** happy.
's = is

Grammar
Possessive adjectives

3 Complete the chart.

Subject pronouns						
I	you	he	she	it	we	they
Possessive adjectives						
my				its	our	

4 Complete the sentences with possessive adjectives.

1 Lucy's dress is black and white, and _____ sandals are brown.
2 Chris's jeans are blue and _____ sweater is gray.
3 Lucy and Nina are happy. They like _____ clothes!
4 I'm wearing a new jacket with _____ jeans.
5 Do you like fashion? What are _____ favorite clothes?

6 Circle the correct answers.

1 Nina's hair is long.
  a 's = possession   b 's = is
2 The boy's jeans are blue.
  a 's = possession   b 's = is
3 He's sad.
  a 's = possession   b 's = is
4 Nina's jacket is new.
  a 's = possession   b 's = is

UNIT 1 What do you like?

Vocabulary
Free-time activities

1 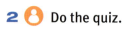 Look at the quiz. Listen and repeat the phrases in blue.

2 Do the quiz.

WHAT KIND OF TEENAGER ARE YOU?

Do the quiz to find out!

1 You have an hour of free time. Do you…
 A) call someone for a chat?
 B) play computer games?
 C) go for a run, walk or ride a bike?

2 It's Friday night. Do you usually…
 A) watch a DVD with a friend?
 B) surf the Internet?
 C) watch the sports channel on TV?

3 On Saturday mornings, do you usually…
 A) go shopping with your friends?
 B) go to a café?
 C) go to the gym, park or sports center?

4 When you go to the beach, do you…
 A) just hang out with your friends?
 B) listen to music or send text messages?
 C) play volleyball or do water sports?

5 It's your birthday. Is your ideal gift…
 A) tickets to go to a theme park with friends?
 B) a smartphone to chat online all the time?
 C) a new bike or skateboard?

6 A friend sends you a text message saying that he/she is very sad and needs to talk to you. Do you…
 A) go to his/her house immediately to help him/her?
 B) keep on exchanging messages with him/her?
 C) advise him/her to go for a walk to feel better?

— SCORE —

Mostly "A"s You're sociable! You're friendly and have a good social life, but you don't go out every night. You can have fun at home, too!
Mostly "B"s You're a technology lover! You're shy and you like being on your own. Don't spend too many hours on your computer, though. Turn it off and go outside!
Mostly "C"s You're active! You're very athletic and you get bored easily. It's great to be fit and healthy, but you must relax and spend time with people sometimes!

12

3 Match adjectives 1–3 from the score box to opposites a–c. Then answer out loud: Do you agree with the result of your quiz?

1 sociable   a lazy
2 friendly   b shy
3 active   c unfriendly

4 What do you usually do on weekends? Complete the chart.

	Saturday	Sunday
mornings	go shopping with Mom	
afternoons		
evenings		

5 In turns, ask and answer about your weekend activities from Activity 4.

— *What do you do on Saturday mornings?*
— *I go shopping with my mom.*

LEARNING TO LEARN

Classifying vocabulary helps you to learn it. Choose one of these options to classify the free-time activities from the text. Activities you...

- like / don't like
- do during the week / on weekends

COMPARING CULTURES

Do teenagers in your country do the same free-time activities as the ones listed in the quiz? What are the cultural activities teens in your country do?

6 Correct the underlined part of the sentences, if necessary. Check (✓) or put a cross (X) next to the them.

1 Alice is not very sociable. She spends most of her free time playing the Internet. ☐
_____
_____

2 How often do you hang out with your friends? ☐
_____
_____

3 I need a new smartphone. This one is too slow to chat text messages. ☐
_____
_____

4 Do you usually listen to music when you are doing your homework? ☐
_____
_____

5 We've never gone to a theme park with our friends. We should do it one of these days. ☐
_____
_____

6 Josh never plays water sports. Actually, he can't swim! ☐
_____
_____

7 In pairs, write another question and three possible answers to include in the quiz.

7 _____
     A) _____.
     B) _____.
     C) _____.

Reading
Posts on a teens website

1 Before you read > Look at the website quickly. What is it about?

---

www.teenweekendaroundtheworld.com

NORTH AMERICA   CENTRAL AMERICA   SOUTH AMERICA   **EUROPE**   AFRICA   ASIA   OCEANIA   SEND A MESSAGE

4 TEEN DAYS OUT IN THE UK

Have you ever felt curious about the activities teenagers in other countries do on the weekend? Here are some messages from teens who live in the UK telling us about their plans for this weekend.

BLUE PLANET AQUARIUM

I always go swimming at the local sports center on Saturday mornings, but this morning I'm swimming with sharks at the Blue Planet Aquarium. It's a great experience! Do you like adventure? Are you good at swimming? Then this is the place for you. First, you must take a diving class, and then, you're ready to swim with the sharks!

RATING 😀 😀   Jack, 13, Stafford

BEAMISH, THE LIVING MUSEUM OF THE NORTH

I usually go shopping downtown on Saturdays, but this Saturday, I'm buying souvenirs in the stores of an old town from the 1900s. I'm actually experiencing life in the past! I'm at Beamish, a "living" museum. At Beamish, you can travel on a tram, have a class at an old village school and much more! I usually hate museums, but Beamish is different!

RATING 😀 😀 😀   Daisy, 14, Durham

THE EDINBURGH GHOST BUS TOUR

My friends and I love horror movies, so here we are – on the Edinburgh Ghost Bus Tour. Edinburgh is a very old city and it is the capital of Scotland. Its past is dark and mysterious, and it has a lot of ghost stories. Our guide is telling us these stories and making lots of funny faces. Actually, the tour isn't scary at all, but we're enjoying it.

RATING 😀 😀   Daniel, 14, Glasgow

THE ADRENALIN QUARRY

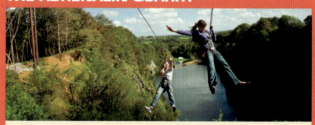

I often go to theme parks with my friends and right now we're at the Adrenalin Quarry, in Cornwall. We're having a lot of fun. Our favorite attraction is the Giant Swing. It's a big swing at the top of a cliff. The swing is very high and really scary. The Adrenalin Quarry is a great theme park. We really recommend it!

RATING 😀 😀 😀   Anna, 15, Cardiff

2 Read for general ideas > Write what you can do at each attraction.

What can you do at the...	
aquarium?	
ghost bus tour?	
museum?	
theme park?	

3 Read for details > Answer the questions.

1. Where does Jack go on Saturday mornings? What is he doing this Saturday morning?
   _____
   _____

2. What kind of movies do Daniel and his friends like? What kind of tour are they taking now?
   _____
   _____

3. Does Daisy like museums? Why does she like Beamish?
   _____
   _____

4. What is the Giant Swing? Where is it?
   _____
   _____

4 Complete the sentences with the places in the box.

> Blue Planet Aquarium   Beamish
> The Edinburgh Ghost Bus Tour
> The Adrenalin Quarry

1. _____ is over a hundred years old.
2. _____ has several attractions.
3. You can learn to dive at the _____.
4. There are dangerous sea animals at the _____.
5. You can go shopping for souvenirs at _____.
6. At _____, you can see what studying in the beginning of the 20th century was like.
7. There is a very scary attraction at _____.
8. There is a guide in _____.

5 If you were in the UK, which of the things on the website would you like to do? Why?
_____
_____

6 In pairs, take turns to ask and answer about your choice in Activity 5.

🟠 *Which of the things would you like to do?*
🔵 *I'd like to visit Beamish.*
🟠 *Why?*
🔵 *Because…*

COMPARING CULTURES

Are there attractions in your country similar to the ones listed on the website? Name two popular attractions for teenagers in your country. What can you do there?

Attraction	What you can do

Find out more information about the attractions.

1. Visit the websites of the attractions mentioned by Daniel, Anna, Jack and Daisy.
2. Find out more information and decide which attraction is the most interesting for teens in your country.
3. Explain your decision to the class.

#tip

To find more information about each place, click on the "Attractions", "Explore" or "More info" tabs.

15

Grammar
Simple present and present progressive

USE

A Analyze these sentences from the text on page 14. <u>Underline</u> three more simple present verb forms and circle two cases of present progressive.

I always <u>go</u> swimming at the local sports center.

This morning I'm swimming in a different place.

Do you like adventure?

My friends and I love horror movies.

I usually hate museums.

We're having a lot of fun.

B Complete the rules with *simple present* or *present progressive*.

We use the _____ to talk about things that are happening now.

We use the _____ to talk about habits or routines.

We use the _____ with *like*, *love*, and *hate*.

C In your notebook, classify these expressions under "simple present" or "present progressive".

sometimes / every day / today / now / often / never / once a week / right now

1 Complete the conversation with the correct form of the verbs in parentheses.

Dan: Hi, Kate! Where (1) _____ (you / go)?

Kate: I (2) _____ (go) to FunLand theme park. (3) _____ (you / know) it?

Dan: Yeah, my brother and I (4) _____ (go / sometimes) there. It's amazing!

Kate: What (5) _____ (be) the best ride?

Dan: I (6) _____ (love) the Dragon Falls. You (7) _____ (get) wet at the end.

Kate: It (8) _____ (sound) cool. Oh, no! It (9) _____ (rain)!

FORM

D Complete the charts.

Simple present – affirmative and negative

I / You / We / They	like / don't like	adventure.
He / She / It	likes / doesn't _____	

Yes/No questions

Do	I / you / we / they	like	adventure?
_____	he / she / it		

Short answers

Yes, / No,	I / you / we / they	do. / _____.
	he / she / it	_____. / doesn't.

Present progressive – affirmative and negative

I	'm / 'm not	
He / She / It	's / _____	swimming.
You / We / They	're / aren't	

Yes/No questions

_____	I	
Is	he / she / it	swimming?
_____	you / we / they	

Short answers

Yes, / No,	I	am. / 'm not.
	he / she / it	_____. / isn't.
	you / we / they	are. / _____.

2 Write questions.

1 What / your parents / do / at the moment?

_____

2 Where / you / usually / go / Friday evenings?

_____

3 What / you / wear / today?

_____

4 What / you / usually / do / after school?

_____

3 🧑 Free practice > In turns, ask and answer the questions from Activity 2. Ask other questions to find out more.

🟡 *What are your parents doing at the moment?*

🔵 *My father is working.*

🟡 *Does he work in an office?*

Vocabulary
Skills and abilities

1 🔊 06 Listen and repeat the words in the box.

> ride a BMX bike   play the drums   sing   climb walls   speak English   dance
> cook   drive a car   draw   paint   understand German   act   jump

2 Look at the website of a TV show. What is the show about?

_____

3 Read the website and complete the sentences with words from Activity 1.

4 👤 In pairs, talk about your skills and abilities. Use words from Activity 1.

🟠 *I can paint very well, but I'm not very good at drawing. How about you?*
🔵 *I can draw and I'm good at painting, too.*

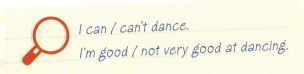

Listening
A TV talent show

5 🔊 07 Listen to part of a TV talent show. Which contestants from Activity 2 are the judges talking to?

_____

6 🔊 07 Listen again. Circle *T* (True) or *F* (False).

1 The first contestant has a strong voice.   T F
2 Zak doesn't have singing lessons.   T F
3 Zak wins this part of the competition.   T F
4 The judges like Ben and Liz.   T F
5 Ben and Liz don't practice every day.   T F
6 Ben and Liz didn't look happy when they were dancing.   T F

Reading
A magazine interview

1 **Before you read >** Look at the interview quickly. Who is the interview with? What is it about?

URBAN SPORTS: A TEEN PERSPECTIVE

DO YOU LIVE IN A CITY? Do you want to do something exciting in your free time? 17-year-old Jon Harrison tells us about urban sports.

REPORTER Jon, first of all, what are urban sports?

JON Urban sports are activities you can do in cities. Skateboarding, BMX biking and parkour – or free running – are all urban sports.

REPORTER Who does them?

JON Teenagers and people in their 20s. Urban sports are popular with young people because they like having fun with their friends and doing something active at the same time.

REPORTER Where do they do these sports?

JON Anywhere! You don't need a special place for urban sports. You can jump or skateboard over walls and you can cycle along roads or down steps. Every city has these things – and they are free!

REPORTER What urban sports do you do?

JON I always do parkour and I sometimes go skateboarding.

REPORTER And what do you wear?

JON Well, you don't need any special clothes. I wear jeans or shorts, T-shirts, and sneakers.

REPORTER Do you practice very often?

JON Well, I love doing parkour, so I practice every day.

REPORTER Do you also practice on cold, rainy days?

JON I don't mind going out on cold days, but I hate getting wet. So I never do parkour on rainy days. Also, it's very dangerous because the surfaces are wet.

REPORTER Do you want to try BMX biking?

JON Yes, I do. Actually, I want a BMX bike for my next birthday. I enjoy doing all kinds of urban sports!

2 **Read for general ideas >** Answer the questions.

1 Where do people do urban sports?

2 Who does urban sports?

3 What urban sports does Jon do?

4 What urban sport does he want to try?

3 **Read for details >** Find:

1 reasons why young people do urban sports.

2 clothes Jon wears for urban sports.

3 a reason why it is not a good idea to do parkour on rainy days.

4 🙂 **Give your opinion >** Do you like urban sports? Do you or your friends do any urban sport?

Grammar
love, hate, (don't) like, don't mind, enjoy + -ing

USE

A Analyze these sentences from the text on page 18. <u>Underline</u> four more verbs that express likes and dislikes and *-ing* forms of verbs.

They <u>like having</u> fun with their friends.

I love doing parkour, so I practice every day.

I don't mind going out on cold days.

I hate getting wet.

I enjoy doing all kinds of urban sports!

B Complete the sentences with *love, hate, like, don't like,* and *don't mind*.

☺☺☺	I _____ swimming.
☺☺	I _____ running.
☺	I _____ painting.
☹	I _____ dancing.
☹☹☹	I _____ singing.

FORM

C Look at the chart.

Expressing likes and dislikes	
I	love hate like don't like don't mind enjoy	dancing.

D <u>Underline</u> the correct options to complete the rules.

- To express likes and dislikes we use *like, enjoy, love,* and *hate* in the **present progressive / simple present** form.
- After *like, enjoy, love,* and *hate* we use the *-ing* **form of verbs / present progressive**.
- *Don't mind* is always used in the **negative / affirmative** form.

1 Circle the correct options.

Ann: What do you like (1) **doing / do** on Saturdays, Lara?
Lara: I (2) **love / don't mind** cycling. It's fun!
Ann: I (3) **hate / like** cycling too, but I don't have a bike. How about taking dance classes?
Lara: Sounds great. I really enjoy (4) **dance / dancing**. There is a hip hop class at the sports center at 8 o'clock.
Ann: At 8 o'clock? I (5) **don't mind / don't like** going to the sports center on Saturdays, but I (6) **love / hate** getting up early.
Lara: Well, there's a class at 11 o'clock.
Ann: That's perfect!

2 Free practice > In pairs, talk about the things you love, like, don't like, don't mind, or hate doing and give reasons why. Use ideas from the boxes.

sing	go to theme parks	dance
watch horror movies	paint
swim	cook	run	climb

| dangerous | I'm good at it. | hard | scary |
| I'm not very good at it. | easy | boring | fun |

🟠 *I hate cooking. I'm not very good at it.*
🔵 *Really? I like cooking. I sometimes help my family to prepare dinner.*

COMPARING LANGUAGES

In English, we use the *-ing* form of verbs after *like, love, hate, enjoy,* and *don't mind*. What happens in your language? Translate these sentences and discuss with your classmates.

I love singing.
I don't mind dancing.
I hate running.

Build your skills

Reading & Listening
An ad

1 Before you read > Look at the ad. What is it about: a sports center, a gym, or an activity camp?

Looking for adventure?

WANTED

Teenagers looking for adventure
Are you 13–16 years old? Do you want to make new friends, do some cool activities and have fun this fall? If the answer is "Yes", then why not spend a weekend in September or October at Greenwood Activity Camp? You'll enjoy two and a half days of adventure, doing your favorite activities and learning amazing new skills.

ACTIVITIES ON OUR ADVENTURE WEEKENDS INCLUDE:

swimming   parkour   singing
sailing   painting   creative writing
skateboarding   photography   … and more!

Price of $150 includes accommodation in log cabins and all meals. Visit our website www.adventureteenscamp.com and sign up today!

2 Read for general ideas > Answer the questions.

1 Who can sign up for an adventure weekend?
   _____
2 When are the adventure weekends?
   _____
3 How long do they last?
   _____
4 How much do they cost?
   _____
5 Where do the teenagers sleep?
   _____

3 Give your opinion > Would you like to go on an adventure weekend? Why (not)? Discuss with your classmates.

4 🔊 08 Listen to a phone conversation about the Greenwood Activity Camp. Which three activities does Owen mention?

_____

5 🔊 08 Listen again. Circle the correct options.

1 Owen thinks the camp is **an interesting** / **a boring** plan.
2 Joe **likes** / **doesn't like** sports.
3 Owen says they can do **the same** / **different** activities at the camp and at school.
4 Joe likes **photography** / **parkour**.
5 Owen is looking at **a website** / **an ad** about the camp.

Listening & Speaking
Asking for personal information

1 Before you listen > Look at the picture. Where is Chris?

_____
_____

2 🔊 09 **Listen for general ideas >** Check (✓) the correct option.

Chris wants to register for:
1 a summer camp. ☐
2 an adventure weekend. ☐
3 a day of adventure. ☐

3 🔊 09 **Listen for details >** Complete the conversation.

Hello. I'd like to (1) _____ for one of your adventure weekends.	OK, great! I just need a few details from you. What's your name?
Chris Bradley.	And what's your address, Chris?
It's (2) _____ .	OK. What's your cell phone (3) _____ ?
(4) _____ .	OK. Do you have an email (5) _____ ?
Yes, it's (6) _____ .	Can you spell that for me?
Yes. It's c-h-r-i-s at i-n-m-a-i-l dot com.	Great, (7) _____ . Oh, I nearly forgot! What's your birthdate?
(8) _____ .	OK, great. Here's a leaflet for you with more (9) _____ about the camp.

4 Speak > Role play in pairs.
1 Role play the conversation in Activity 3.
2 Role play a new conversation. Give your personal information.
3 Switch roles.

Keep it going!

Circle these words in the conversation.
    And...   OK.   Yes.
    OK, great.   Great, thanks.

Remember to use them to sound natural.

Writing
A personal profile

1 Read Claire's profile. Why doesn't Claire like singing? Why does she have a lot of purple clothes?

Claire Edwards

Hi! My name's Claire Edwards and I'm 14 years old. I'm from Providence in Rhode Island, in the United States. I live with my mom and dad and my 12-year-old brother Sam. My best friends are Holly and Anita.

I love music. I listen to music all the time and I play the guitar in a band with some of my friends. We're called The Daisies and we play rock and pop music. I write the songs, but I don't like singing because I'm shy. I'm writing a new song at the moment.

I also love going shopping because I'm really into fashion. My favorite color is purple, so I have lots of purple clothes. I'm not very active, but I sometimes go rollerblading in the park.

2 Read the "Write it right!" section.

Write it right!
Giving reasons

➔ We use **because** when we give a reason for something.

I also love going shopping because I'm really into fashion.

➔ We use **so** when we talk about the result of something.

My favorite color is purple, so I have lots of purple clothes.

3 Complete these sentences with *because* or *so*.
1. I'm an animal lover, _____ I have lots of pets.
2. I like dancing _____ it's fun!
3. I love music, _____ I play in a band.
4. I don't go to pop concerts _____ I'm too young.

Writing task

Plan > In your notebook, make notes about your:
- name, age, and country
- family and friends
- likes and reasons
- dislikes and reasons

Write > Write your personal profile. Remember to use:
- vocabulary from pages 12 and 17.
- the simple present for routines.
- the present progressive for actions happening now.
- *because* to give reasons and *so* to talk about results.

Check > Check your writing.

The Beat MAGAZINE

What does your bedroom say about you?

What are your favorite possessions? The objects in your bedroom tell a lot about your personality and your likes. Read about John and Lara. Are their rooms similar to yours?

John MacLean, 13

Lara Holmes, 14

When you walk into 13-year-old John MacLean's bedroom, it's clear that he's soccer crazy. There's a soccer ball by the bed. On the wall, there's a signed Chelsea jersey and two pictures. In one of them, John is playing soccer at the club and in the other, he's watching a soccer game with his friends at the Chelsea stadium.

"When I get home from school, I come to my room and I play soccer video games on my Xbox. I have a TV in my room. I also have all my *Harry Potter* books and some soccer magazines. I enjoy being in my bedroom because all my favorite possessions are here."

John has a passion for soccer and his room shows it!

"My room is small, but I don't mind. I think it's perfect. I have a desk and a laptop. It's new and I love it because I can surf the Internet or chat with my friends online," says 14-year-old Lara Holmes. She admits she likes talking to her friends at all times!

When you look around the room, you can see a lot of pictures on the walls, a bookcase full of books and many framed pictures of her family and friends.

"That is my best friend, Kay," says Lara, pointing to the picture of a girl with long dark hair. "And this is my friend Brad." She holds up a framed picture of a boy.

It's clear that Lara is a very friendly teenager. "My friends are my treasure," she says.

1 🔊 10 Listen and read about John and Lara. What do they have in their bedrooms?

_____
_____
_____

2 Read again and answer the questions.

1 What is John's favorite sport?
_____

2 What is John doing in the pictures on the wall?
_____
_____

3 What does he like reading?
_____

4 Why does Lara love her laptop?
_____
_____

5 Who is Kay?
_____

6 What can you say about Lara's personality?
_____

3 👤 Choose one of these activities.

1 In your notebook, write eight sentences about John or Lara. For each sentence, write a new sentence about you.

2 Draw a mind map about each text in your notebook. Compare mind maps with a classmate.

UNIT 2 Music and TV

Vocabulary
Music

1 Look at the *What's on?* guide. What concerts are there in May? Which concert do you prefer?

WHAT'S ON?

FRIDAY MAY 6TH
Justin Timberlake
The American pop and R&B singer comes to town with a great concert, in the world tour of his new album.

SATURDAY MAY 14TH
Maroon 5
The American pop-rock band in concert. With Adam on vocals, James on guitar, Mickey on bass, Matt on drums, and PJ and Jesse on keyboards.

THURSDAY MAY 19TH
YOA Orchestra of the Americas
Young musicians aged 18–30 from 25 countries of the Americas bring the best classical music to this spring's Music Festival.

SUNDAY MAY 29TH
Shakira
Everybody sings and dances to the songs of the Colombian popstar. She also plays the guitar and the harmonica in most concerts.

2 🔊 11 Listen and repeat the words in the chart.

Kinds of music	Instruments	Musicians
pop	piano	singer
dance	bass	choir
classical	guitar	backing vocals
latin	keyboard	band
rock	drums	orchestra
rap	violin	composer
rhythm and blues (R&B)	harmonica	conductor

3 Read the guide and answer the questions.

1 What kinds of music does Justin Timberlake sing?
_____

2 Who is Maroon 5's singer?
_____

3 What instruments do the members of the band play?
_____

4 How old are the members of YOA?
_____

5 Where are they from?
_____

6 What kind of music do they play?
_____

7 Where is Shakira from?
_____

8 What musical instruments does she play?
_____

LEARNING TO LEARN

To learn new words, you have to use them. Choose musicians, singers and bands and write five sentences about them.

musician	sentence

4 Order the words to make questions. Then write answers that are true for you.

1 favorite / what's / pop / song / your / ?
_____
_____

2 you / the / can / play / guitar / ?
_____
_____

3 like / classical / do / music / you / ?
_____
_____

4 rock / your / singer / who's / favorite / ?
_____
_____

5 band / your / favorite / what's / ?
_____
_____

5 In turns, ask and answer about your favorite kind of music, and your favorite band, song and singer.

🟠 *What's your favorite kind of music?*
🔵 *I really like dance music.*

25

Reading
A magazine article

1 Before you read > Look at the pictures. What are the people in the images doing?

_____

_____

The Beat Magazine

Amazing music!

THE LIVERPOOL SIGNING CHOIR

The members of the Liverpool Signing Choir don't sing – they "sign"! They are a special choir because many of its members are deaf. They can't hear, so they can't use their voices. But they can use their hands, so they sing with sign language.

Conductor Catherine Hegarty formed this choir at an elementary school in Liverpool in 2001. When she started it, it had 12 members. It was an after-school club. Today, there are about 100 young people in the choir. They are aged 7–24.

Some years ago, The Liverpool Signing Choir performed for the Queen when she visited Liverpool. In 2009, they went to London and performed at Wembley Stadium. In 2012, when millions of people listened to them at the London Olympic Games, they became famous.

STOMP

The British group uses everyday objects and their bodies to create music and dance, in sparkling performances. Steve McNicholas and Luke Cresswell founded the percussion group in Brighton, in the UK, in 1991, and staged its first show in the summer of that year.

After enormous success in the UK, STOMP traveled around the world with its show. Between 1991 and 1994, they went to Hong Kong, Dublin, Barcelona, Sydney, and other

cities. After that, they became famous worldwide.

But the most important moment in their career was in 2012. They performed to millions of people at the closing ceremony of the London Olympic Games.

McNicholas and Cresswell didn't think STOMP would be so successful! Nowadays, STOMP's expanded cast performs in New York and in London, and there is also a cast on a world tour. Each show lasts about one hour and 45 minutes.

2 Read for general ideas > Complete the sentences.

1 The Liverpool Signing Choir is special because many of its members _____ .
2 These members sing _____ .
3 _____ formed this choir at an _____ .
4 The choir became famous when _____ .
5 STOMP is a _____ group from the _____ .
6 Steve McNicholas and _____ founded the group more than 20 years ago.
7 They traveled around the world, performing in Hong Kong, _____ , Barcelona and _____ in the 1990s.
8 Nowadays, there are shows in _____ , _____ , and a cast on a world tour.

3 Read for details > Find these numbers in the text. Then match them to the information they refer to.

1	1991	a	the Liverpool Signing Choir members' ages
2	1994	b	the year that the choir started
3	2001	c	the number of members of the choir today
4	2009	d	the year that they became famous
5	2012	e	the number of members when the choir started
6	7–24	f	the year that they were at Wembley
7	12	g	the year that STOMP performed for the first time
8	100	h	the year that they finished their first world tour
9	1h45	i	the duration of STOMP's show

4 Read for details > Write two facts the Liverpool Signing Choir and STOMP have in common.

1 _____
2 _____

5 Read for inference > Who could have said the quotes below? Complete.

> Alan Asuncion, a member of STOMP
> Catherine Hegarty
> Luke Cresswall
> Mrs. Taylor, mother of Lukas, a choir singer
> Mia, a big fan of STOMP
> Danielle, a member of the choir

1 "I'm very proud of the singers and their work. I love being their conductor."
_____

2 "My 7-year-old son is so happy now. Singing helped him to socialize and make new friends."
_____

3 "Steve and I met about 30 years ago. I played the drums in a band and Steve worked as an actor."
_____

4 "I can't believe I got tickets to see my favorite percussion group in London. I'm so excited!"
_____

5 "I joined the group in 2007. I'm so thankful to perform in my favorite Off-Broadway show."
_____

6 "I was very shy before I met Ms. Hegarty and the other members. Singing changed my life."
_____

Find out more about the Liverpool Signing Choir or YOA.

1 Use the keywords "Liverpool Signing Choir" or "YOA Orchestra of the Americas."
2 Watch videos of live performances.
3 Tell the class your opinion on the performances.

#tip

Choose videos or find videos on official websites.

Grammar
Simple past – regular and irregular verbs (1): affirmative and negative

USE

A Analyze these sentences from the text on page 26. Underline eight more simple past verb forms.

Catherine Hegarty <u>formed</u> this choir at an elementary school.

When she started it, it had 12 members.

Some years ago, the choir performed for the Queen when she visited Liverpool.

In 2009, they went to London.

STOMP traveled around the world with its show.

After that, they became famous worldwide.

McNicholas and Cresswell didn't think STOMP would be so successful!

B Check (✓) the time expressions we can use with the simple past.

- in 2009 ☐
- two years ago ☐
- last night / year ☐
- now ☐
- yesterday ☐
- at the moment ☐

1 Complete the text with the correct form of the verbs in parentheses.

Not long ago, people (1) _____ (not listen) to portable music. They (2) _____ (not have) MP3 players – they (3) _____ (have) record players. Portable music players (4) _____ (become) popular in 1980, when Sony (5) _____ (invent) the Walkman. In 2001, Apple (6) _____ (make) a new portable music player – the iPod. People (7) _____ (love) it!

2 👤 Free practice › Use verbs and time expressions from the boxes to write sentences that are true for you in your notebook. Remember to use the simple past.

FORM

C Complete the chart.

Affirmative		
I / You / He / She / It / We / They	**visited**	London.
	went	to London.
Negative		
I / You / He / She / It / We / They	**didn't** ____	London.
	____ **go**	to London.

D Look at the chart in Activity C and answer the questions.

1 *Visit* is a regular verb. What is the simple past ending for regular verbs?
_____

2 *Go* is an irregular verb. What is its simple past form?
_____

3 How do we form the simple past negative? Is it different for regular and irregular verbs?
_____

E Classify the verbs from Activity A in your notebook.

regular verbs	irregular verbs
visit – visited	go – went

F Look at these simple past verbs. Add them to the charts in Activity E.

watched / played / made / finished / liked / loved / did

have breakfast	listen to music
start school	watch TV
go to the movies	go on vacation

this morning	last night
last week	yesterday
at... o'clock	... months ago

COMPARING LANGUAGES

In English, the simple past form does not change for different subject pronouns. What happens in your language?

28

Vocabulary
TV programs

1 🔊 12 Look at the TV guide. Say the names of the TV programs. Then listen and repeat the words in the box.

> reality show   talk show   soap opera
> the news   sports program   comedy
> cartoon   documentary   movie   drama
> music program   game show

2 Read the TV guide. Find and underline one example of each of these programs.

1 a music program
2 a soap opera
3 a movie
4 a sports program
5 a drama
6 a cartoon

3 👤 Answer the questions orally. Use the words from the box.

> boring   scary   fantastic
> terrible   funny

1 What kinds of TV programs do you like? Why?
2 What is your favorite TV program? Why?
3 What kinds of programs don't you like? Why?

Listening
What was on?

4 🔊 13 Listen to the conversation and complete the sentences.

1 Hazel watched _____ on _____ at _____ o'clock.
2 James watched a _____ called _____.

5 🔊 13 Listen again. Circle the correct options.

1 Hazel and James are chatting at the **bus stop / train station**.
2 Hazel is going **to her friend's house / home**.
3 It is James's **sister's / mom's** birthday today.
4 The program that Hazel watched was **boring / fantastic**.
5 The program that James watched was **terrible / scary**.

CBC

4:00 p.m. Crazy Kids!
All our favorite cartoon characters

5:00 p.m. Life in the Wild
Documentary about penguins in the Antarctic

5:45 p.m. The Mark Spencer Show
Talk show guests include hip hop star Def Jam

7:15 p.m. Top of the Charts
The Friday night music program

8:00 p.m. CSI
Another exciting episode of this famous crime drama

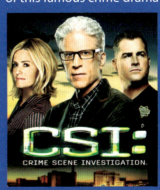

9:00 p.m. The Big Bang Theory
Double comedy – two episodes

MBC

4:00 p.m. Neighbors
Sophie gets good news in today's episode of the Australian soap opera.

5:00 p.m. Who Wants To Be A Millionaire?
More difficult questions for the game show contestants

6:00 p.m. The News at 6
National and regional news

7:00 p.m. Olympic Stars
The sports program that follows USA's top athletes.

8:00 p.m. New Dawn
Movie directed by Bart Samson. Amy Lee stars in this exciting drama.

10:30 p.m. I'm a Celebrity…
The reality show where celebrities have to eat insects!

Reading
TV programs reviews

1 Before you read > Look at the website. What is it about?

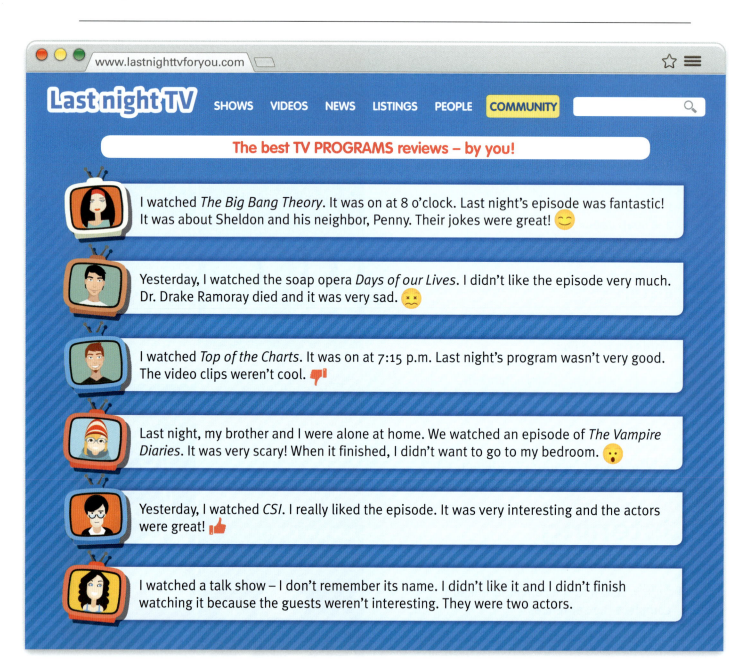

2 Read for general ideas > Complete the chart.

TV program	Good or bad?

3 Read for details > Match 1–6 to the adjectives.

1 the jokes in *The Big Bang Theory*
2 the *Days of our Lives* episode
3 the video clips on *Top of the Charts*
4 the episode of *The Vampire Diaries*
5 the episode of *CSI*
6 the guests of the talk show

a interesting
b scary
c not cool
d sad
e great
f not interesting

Grammar

Be – simple past: affirmative and negative

USE

A Analyze these sentences from the text on page 30. <u>Underline</u> eight more examples of the simple past form of *be*.

Last night's episode <u>was</u> fantastic.

Their jokes were great!

It was very sad.

Last night's program wasn't very good.

The video clips weren't cool.

Last night, my brother and I were alone at home.

It was very scary.

The actors were great.

The guests weren't interesting.

B Look at the sentences in Activity A again. Find and write an example for each rule.

We use the simple past of *be*:

- + descriptions of people: _____
  _____
- + descriptions of things: _____
  _____
- + places: _____
  _____

1 Write a negative and an affirmative sentence. Use *was* or *were*.

1 The story / good / terrible
_____

2 My friends / at the movies / at a party
_____

3 We / at the beach / in the mountains
_____

4 She / in my house / at school
_____

FORM

C Complete the charts.

Affirmative		
Singular		
I / He / She / It	was	at home.
You	were	
Plural		
We / You / They	_____	at home.

Negative		
Singular		
I / He / She / It	_____	funny.
You	weren't	
Plural		
We / You / They	_____	funny.

D Answer the questions.

1 Are *wasn't* and *weren't* full forms or short forms?
_____

2 What are their full forms?
wasn't: _____
weren't: _____

2 Free practice › Use words from the boxes and your own ideas to write true sentences about a movie in your notebook. Remember to use the simple past of *be*.

the music	the special effects
the actors	the story	the ending
the jokes	the action scenes

| cool | boring | fun | good |
| great | fantastic | funny | terrible |

COMPARING LANGUAGES

Translate into your language:
They were at home.
The actors were good.
What are the two meanings of the verb *be*?

Build your skills

Reading & Listening
A bulletin board

1 Before you read > Look at the bulletin board. What are the posters about?

2 Read > Answer the questions.

1. What movie can you watch on the Movie Night?

2. What can you do on the Talent Show?

3. When is the Party Night?

4. What time do people meet for the Trip Night?

3 Give your opinion > Look at the information again. Which night do you prefer? Why? Discuss with your classmates.

4 🔊 14 Listen to Chloe's phone conversation. Where is Chloe? Where is Lisa?

5 🔊 14 Listen again. Choose the correct options.

1. Lisa is **watching TV** / **doing her homework**.
2. Chloe **is** / **isn't** having a good time.
3. Lisa wants to **go shopping** / **play tennis** tomorrow.
4. They agree to meet at **11:00 a.m.** / **11:30 a.m.**
5. It's **Party Night** / **Movie Night** at the youth club.

Listening & Speaking
Talking about likes and dislikes

1 Before you listen > Look at the picture of Ben and Chloe. Where are they? What are they talking about?

_____

_____

2 🔊 15 Listen for general ideas > Answer the questions.

1 What is the playlist for?

_____

2 How many songs do they choose?

_____

3 Listen for details > Complete the conversation.

Let's think about the song (1) _____ for the Party Night.	Yes, (2) _____ !
Do you like Will Robins?	Yes, I (3) _____ him!
What's your favorite (4) _____ ? How about *Players*?	No, I prefer *Love*.
OK, that's (5) _____ . I like that, too.	And what about Bankside? Do you like them?
(6) _____ . I can't stand them!	Really? What else do you like, then?
I (7) _____ Finn Woods. They're better than Bankside.	OK. I don't mind Finn Woods. Which (8) _____ do you like best?
I really like *Living there*. That's quite (9) _____ .	Great! And let's have something by Bright Things, too.
Yes. How about *Gems*?	(10) _____ ! OK. We have three songs so far!

4 Speak > Role play in pairs.
1. Role play the conversation in Activity 3.
2. Role play a new conversation. Choose bands, singers and songs you like.
3. Switch roles.

Keep it going!

Underline these phrases in the conversation.

I like...   I prefer...
I really like...   I don't mind...   I can't stand...
Let's...   How about...?   ... what about...?

Remember to use them to talk about preferences and to make suggestions.

33

Writing
A short biography

1 Read the biography. Who is Taylor Swift? When did she become famous?

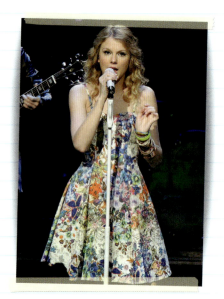

Taylor Swift is a famous American singer and musician. She plays the guitar, the piano and the ukulele. Her favorite type of music is country.

When Taylor was a child, she didn't like school. She loved music. She started playing the guitar when she was 12 years old. Then she started writing songs. When she was 14, her family moved to Nashville – the home of country music. She really liked this kind of music!

In 2006, at the age of 16, Taylor recorded her first album, "Taylor Swift," and she became famous. Two years later, she recorded her second album, "Fearless." In 2009, she performed in North America and Europe, and the following year, she went to Australia and Asia. In 2010, she won four Grammy Awards for her album "Fearless." Taylor made her third album in 2010 and her fourth album in 2012. Her fifth album came out in 2014. They were all a great success!

2 Read the "Write it right!" section.

Write it right!
Past time expressions

⇢ Use past time expressions to refer to past events.

She started playing the guitar **when she was 12 years old**.

Two years later, she recorded her second album.

In 2006, at the age of 16, Taylor recorded her first album.

3 Read the biography again. Underline three more examples of past time expressions.

4 Analyze these sentences and answer: Where in the sentence do we generally write time expressions? When do we use a comma? Discuss with your classmates.

1 In 2006, she recorded her first album.
2 She recorded her first album in 2006.
3 She didn't like school when she was a child.
4 When she was a child, she didn't like school.

Writing task

Plan > Choose a famous musician. Find out about his/her life and, in your notebook, make notes about:
- country of origin
- instruments and kind of music
- childhood
- start of his/her career
- when he/she became famous
- albums and awards

Write > Write the biography. Remember to use:
- the simple present for present habits or routines.
- the simple past for past events.
- past time expressions.

Check > Check your writing.

34

The Beat MAGAZINE

Professor Brian Cox

Do you like physics, the solar system, or rock music? Then read about Brian Cox, a very special scientist.

Brian Cox didn't start his career in an ordinary way. His first job wasn't in a laboratory. It was with a band!

Everything started when Brian was in his twenties. One night, he went to a concert with his sister. A band performed on stage and he loved it, so he decided to be a rock star. In 1986, he became the keyboard player for a rock band called Dare and they recorded two albums. Then he joined another band, D:Ream, and they had a hit single and became famous.

At that time, Brian started studying physics at university and he discovered a new ambition: he wanted to be a scientist. He was a brilliant student and, in 2009, he became Professor of Particle Physics at the University of Manchester. Today, he works at the CERN laboratory in Geneva, Switzerland.

Brian is also a very good TV and radio host. In 2010, he started hosting the television series *The Wonders of the Solar System* on the BBC – a famous British TV channel – and it was a great success. A lot of people watched his programs because they were very interesting. Today, his new science programs are very popular, too.

Professor Brian Cox inspires students all over the world to study science. He loves studying the planets and outer space. He believes that outer space can help us to understand life on Earth.

---

1 🔊 **16** Listen and read about Professor Brian Cox. What is special about him?

_____

2 Read again and circle *T* (True), *F* (False) or *NM* (Not Mentioned).

1 He became a rock star at the age of 30. **T F NM**
2 He played the keyboards for a jazz band. **T F NM**
3 D:Ream wasn't a popular band. **T F NM**
4 Brian had a lot of friends at university. **T F NM**
5 People liked his TV programs. **T F NM**
6 Brian loves studying the galaxies. **T F NM**
7 He wants to travel to outer space. **T F NM**

3 👤 Choose one of these activities.

1 Write a summary of the text in your notebook. Include the main ideas.
2 In your notebook, write a list of facts that surprised you about Brian Cox. Compare lists with a classmate.

35

Vocabulary

Free-time activities

1 Complete the sentences with the verbs from the box.

> send   chat   do   hang   go   surfing

1. On weekends, I usually _____ out with friends.
2. I spend a lot of time on my computer. I love _____ the Internet.
3. I don't usually talk on my cell phone, but I always _____ text messages.
4. Do you _____ water sports in summer?
5. I use my laptop every day. I do my homework and I _____ online at the same time.
6. They sometimes _____ for a swim.

☐ / 6 points

Skills and abilities

2 Complete the sentences with the verbs from the box.

> draw   climb   understand   ride   cook   drive

1. I can _____ a bike, but I can't _____ a car.
2. We can _____ spaghetti.
3. She can _____ beautiful pictures of animals.
4. I can _____ Italian, but I can't speak it.
5. He does parkour. He can jump from walls. He can _____ them, too.

☐ / 6 points

Grammar

Simple present and present progressive

3 Write sentences or questions. Use the simple present.

1. he / go to the gym / every day ✗
_____

2. they / always / watch DVDs / Fridays ✓
_____

3. she / often / do urban sports ?
_____

☐ / 3 points

4 Write sentences or questions. Use the present progressive.

1. I / wear / jeans / today ✓
_____

2. you / enjoy / the tour ?
_____

3. he / listen to music / right now ✗
_____

☐ / 3 points

5 Complete the sentences with the correct form of the verbs in parentheses.

1. She usually _____ (meet) her friends on weekends, but today is Saturday and she _____ (study) for her exams.
2. They _____ (run) in the park right now, but they _____ (not usually go) for a run on Fridays.
3. He _____ (not play) video games now. He only _____ (play) video games when his friends are online.

☐ / 6 points

love, hate, (don't) like, don't mind, enjoy

6 Circle the correct options.

Ben: Do you want to join an after-school club?
Kim: Good idea. I (1) **love / hate** singing. How about joining the choir?
Ben: The choir? I can't sing very well. And I hate (2) **practice / practicing** songs for hours.
Kim: OK. Can you play a musical instrument?
Ben: Oh no, I can't. I (3) **enjoy / don't like** listening to music, but I can't play it.
Kim: Well, there's a drama club. Do you enjoy (4) **act / acting**?
Ben: I (5) **hate / don't mind** acting, but I don't like (6) **act / acting** in public.

☐ / 6 points

Total Score: ☐ / 30 points

Vocabulary
Music

1 Complete the words related to music.

1 She makes music. She's a c_____.
2 She's a member of a band. She's on the k_____.
3 She sings in a band. She's a s_____.
4 He directs the musicians of an orchestra. He's a c_____.
5 This kind of music is great to dance to. It's d_____ music.

6 He's playing the d_____.

7 These people are singing in a c_____.

☐ / 7 points

TV programs

2 Complete the words for TV programs.

1 This program is about animals, people in history, or important events:
___ ___ ___ ___m___ ___ ___a___ ___ ___
2 On this kind of program, you can watch celebrities in everyday life:
___ ___ ___l___ ___ ___ ___h___ ___
3 This program is about the imaginary lives of fictional characters:
___o___ ___ o___ ___ ___ ___
4 This program makes you laugh:
___ ___ ___ ___ ___y
5 On this kind of program, a person interviews famous people:
___ ___ ___k ___ ___o___

☐ / 5 points

Grammar
Simple past – regular and irregular verbs (1)

3 Complete the sentences with the simple past form of the verbs in parentheses.

1 When Taylor Swift _____ (be) a child, she _____ (have) a guitar and she practiced in her house.
2 Last week, I _____ (go) to the movies. I _____ (not like) the movie. It _____ (be) long and boring. It _____ (start) at 6:00 p.m. and _____ (finish) at 9:15 p.m.
3 Justin Bieber _____ (not be) 16 years old when he _____ (record) his first album. He was 15!
4 I _____ (watch) a comedy last night. The actors _____ (not be) famous, but they _____ (be) very funny.

☐ / 12 points

4 Complete the text with the simple past form of the verbs from the box.

| perform | be (x2) | play | not have | become |

Ludwig van Beethoven (1) _____ a German musician. He never married and he (2) _____ any children. He (3) _____ the piano, the organ, and the violin. He (4) _____ in public for the first time at the age of 5. His compositions (5) _____ great. He (6) _____ deaf at the age of 30.

☐ / 6 points

Check your performance!

 Try again! 0–9
 Keep up! 10–16
 Well done! 17–23
 Great job! 24–30

Total Score: ☐ / 30 points

UNIT 3 Fact or fiction?

Vocabulary
Types of books

1 Look at the website. What is it about? Do you know similar websites?

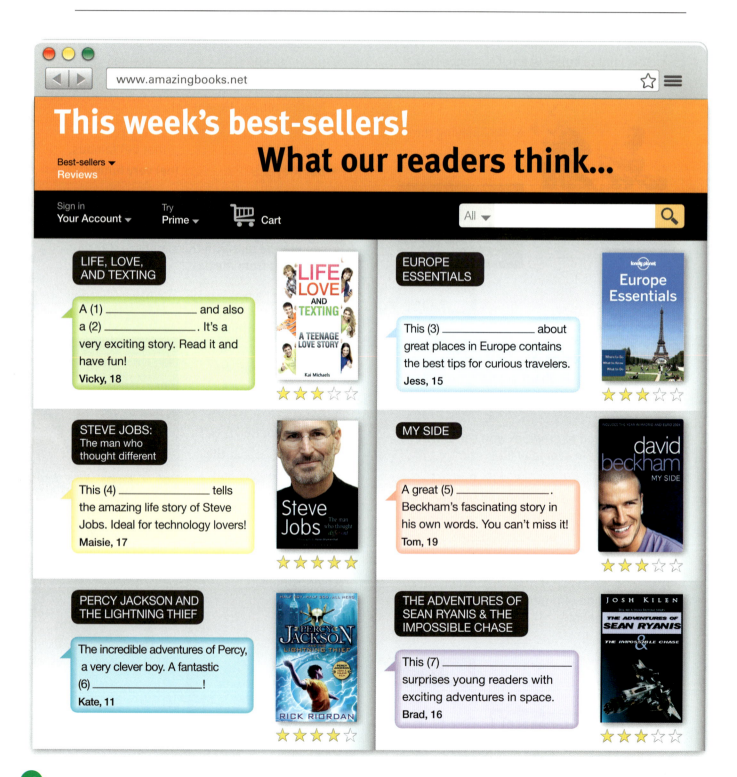

UNIT 3

2 🔊 17 Listen and repeat. Then complete the information on the website with words from the box.

> adventure story   autobiography   biography
> comic novel   cookbook   detective novel
> fairy tale   historical novel   poetry book
> romantic novel   science fiction novel
> thriller   travel guide

3 Find words in Activity 2 that refer to:

1 a story about trying to solve a crime.
   _____

2 a traditional story about magical events.
   _____

3 a book that helps you to make food.
   _____

4 an exciting story, often about danger or crime.
   _____

5 a fiction book about people and events in the past.
   _____

6 a book with poems.
   _____

4 Look at the website again. Complete the sentences.

1 The subtitle of the romantic novel:
   _____

2 The main character of the adventure story:
   _____

3 The world region covered in the travel guide:
   _____

4 The best book for people who like technology:
   _____

5 The author of the autobiography
   _____

5 Read the book titles that appear on the public library's list. Complete the list with the words from the box.

> cookbook   detective novel   fairy tale
> poetry book   romantic novel
> science fiction novel   travel guide

Most borrowed books
Greenville Public Library

1 *Love in a Rainy Afternoon*
By Samantha Ellis
Genre: _____

2 *Crime on Oak Street*
By Lisa Brown
Genre: _____

3 *The Princess, the Maid and the Magic Ring*
By Lukas Clark
Genre: _____

4 *Journey to Mars*
By Andrew Taylor
Genre: _____

5 *The Budget Traveler*
By Katie Spencer
Genre: _____

6 *100 Recipes from Indian Cuisine*
By Maya Sodhi
Genre: _____

7 *365 – A poem a day*
By various authors
Genre: _____

6 👤 In turns, say which of the books from the website you would / wouldn't like to read. Explain why. Use words from the box.

> exciting   interesting   funny   fun
> long   boring   useful

🟠 I'd like to read *My Side* because I love autobiographies.

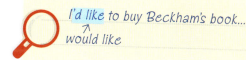

LEARNING TO LEARN
To learn categories of words, personalize them by writing down your own examples:

Fairy tale: Cinderella, Peter Pan, …

Reading
An online message board

1 Before you read > Look at the message board. What is it about?

---

www.topreadingideas.com

MESSAGE BOARD   FAQs Register Login   Go

Reading ideas for your vacation!

Post reply | 4 posts | Page 1 of 1

Were you on vacation last year? Where were you? Tell us about a book you read. Was it good? Was it bad? Were the characters interesting?

Roxy, 13

by **Roxy** Wed Jan 12 6:12 p.m.

I was at the beach on my last vacation. I read *The Adventures of Sean Ryanis* and I really enjoyed it. It was about a boy and his adventures in space. It was very exciting. I think it is a great book. I recommend it!

Comments: 3

Tony, 16

by **Tony** Wed Jan 12 7:27 p.m.

I read the biography of Steve Jobs on my last vacation. Jobs was a very important man in the history of technology. His ideas were brilliant. Steve and his team invented the Apple computer, the iPod, and the iPhone. He also formed Pixar. This company made the animated movies *Toy Story, Monsters Inc*, and *Finding Nemo*. Steve Jobs was an incredible man. You must read this book. It's very interesting!

Comments: 2

Lucy, 15

by **Lucy** Thu Jan 13 8:42 p.m.

My family and I like traveling and visiting new places. We were in Europe last year and we used the travel guide *Europe Essentials* every day of our trip. It was very useful. The book contains a lot of information, but you don't need to read it all. You can read the parts that you are interested in.

Comments: 2

Matt, 12

By **Matt** Thu Jan 13 8:53 p.m.

I always read during my vacation. Adventure stories are my favorite books. On my vacation last year, I read *Terror on Mount Everest*. It was about two climbers. They were on Mount Everest and they met the Yeti monster. The characters weren't interesting and the story wasn't exciting. It was long and boring. I don't recommend it.

Comments: 1

Emily, 13

By **Emily** Thu Jan 13 9:21 p.m.

I love reading, and not only when I'm on vacation. Last year I went to my grandma's house in the country, and there aren't many things to do there, so I read… a lot! Most books were nice, but I'll tell you which book NOT to read: *Love in a Rainy Afternoon*. This story is so boring! The characters were not interesting at all!

Comments: 4

UNIT 3

2 Read for general ideas > Complete the chart.

	Book	Good or bad?	Why?
Roxy			
Tony			
Lucy			
Matt			
Emily			

3 Read for details > Answer the questions.

1 Where was Roxy on her last vacation?

_____

2 What were some of Steve Jobs and his team's inventions?

_____

3 What are the names of some famous movies by Pixar?

_____

4 Where were Lucy and her family last year?

_____

5 What are Matt's favorite books?

_____

6 What is *Terror on Mount Everest* about?

_____

_____

7 Where was Emily on her last vacation?

_____

8 Were there many things to do there?

_____

4 Read for inference > Match the comments to the posts on the message board.

1 Roxy's post
2 Tony's post
3 Lucy's post
4 Matt's post
5 Emily's post

by Melinda Fri Jan 14 1:05 p.m.

How come you didn't like it??? It's the most romantic book ever <3!!! You don't know what you're talking about… ☐

by Marissa Fri Jan 14 2:21 p.m.

This guide is just great! It's so easy to find the information you need and the maps are clear and accurate. ☐

by Meghan Fri Jan 14 3:35 p.m.

If you like this kind of book I recommend *The Innovators: How a Group of Hackers, Geniuses, and Geeks Created the Digital Revolution*, by Walter Isaacson. ☐

by Liam Fri Jan 14 5:15 p.m.

I love Josh Kilen's books! He's a great science fiction writer. I'm reading another book he wrote, based on Minecraft. It's really good! ☐

by Jake Fri Jan 14 6:12 p.m.

You're right about this book, it's really bad… I just couldn't read it until the end. Who believes in Bigfoot anyway? ☐

5 Personalize > Write a post about a book you read.

41

Grammar
Be – simple past: questions

USE

A Analyze these questions from the text on page 40. <u>Underline</u> four more examples of the simple past of *be*.

1 <u>Were</u> you on vacation last year?
2 Where were you?
3 Was it good?
4 Was it bad?
5 Were the characters interesting?

B Match these answers to the questions in Activity A.

- We were in Europe. ☐
- Yes, it It was great! ☐
- Yes, it was. It was long and boring. ☐
- Yes, they were. ☐
- Yes, I was. ☐

1 Write questions. Use the simple past of *be*. Then complete the short answers.

1 Steve Jobs / an actor?
_____
No, he _____ .

2 they / at the beach?
_____
No, they _____ .

3 she / at school?
_____
Yes, she _____ .

4 the stories / good?
_____
Yes, they _____ .

2 👤 Think about a book you enjoyed reading and answer the questions.

1 What was its title?
_____

2 Who was its author?
_____

FORM

C Complete the chart.

Yes/No questions			
_____	I / he / she / it		in Europe?
Were	you / we / they		
Short answers			
Yes,	I / he / she / it	was.	
	you / we / they	_____.	
No,	I / he / she / it	wasn't.	
	you / we / they	_____.	
Wh- questions			
Where	_____	you / they?	
	_____	he / she / it?	

D Compare the word order of statements and questions. Write new examples in a new diagram in your notebook.

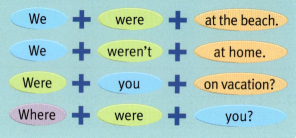

3 What type of book was it?
_____

4 Explain why you liked it.
_____

3 Complete the questions with *was* or *were*.

1 Where _____ you last summer?
2 Who _____ your first teacher?
3 When _____ your last birthday?
4 What _____ your favorite subjects last year?
5 Where _____ you at 8 o'clock this morning?

4 👤 Free practice ▸ In turns, ask and answer the questions in Activity 3.

COMPARING LANGUAGES

In English, the word order of questions with *was* and *were* is different from the word order of statements. What happens in your language?

Vocabulary
Verbs to talk about people's lives in the past

1 Look at the pictures in the quiz. Do you know these people? Discuss with your classmates.

2 🔊 18 Look at the timeline. Listen and repeat the words in blue. Then do the quiz.

AMAZING PEOPLE QUIZ
Do you know these people? Who are they?

1950

1962 A black man went to prison and **spent** almost 27 years there because he **thought** discrimination was wrong. Later, he became the president of his country.

1963 An American man **opened** a theme park in Florida, USA. He **produced** many movies for children.

1980 A famous musician **died** in New York. A fan **killed** him. He **wished** to live in a world of peace.

2006 An Italian man **gave** his last performance. He was one of the best opera singers in the world.

2004 A young man **created** Facebook in his room at university. He was 20 years old. He **earned** millions of dollars.

1993 An American movie producer made the first *Jurassic Park* movie. It had great special effects. Millions of people **saw** it around the world.

2007 A British writer **wrote** her seventh book, which **sold** about 100 million copies. People **bought** it because the story was great.

2009 A teenager **began** her sailing trip around the world. She **finished** it seven months later. She was 16 years old!

NOW

a JK Rowling b John Lennon

c Nelson Mandela d Mark Zuckerberg

e Steven Spielberg

f Luciano Pavarotti

g Jessica Watson

h Walt Disney

3 👤 Play a memory game in pairs. You mention a fact from the quiz and your classmate says the person's name. Then switch roles.
- 🟠 *He made Jurassic Park.*
- 🔵 *Steven Spielberg!*

Listening
Famous people in modern history

4 🔊 19 Listen to a reporter interviewing some people. Which names from the quiz do they mention?

_____

5 🔊 19 Listen again. Answer the questions.

1 What is today's program about?
_____

2 Who is Sam Jenkins?
_____

3 Why does the woman choose John Lennon?
_____
_____

4 Why does the man choose Mark Zuckerberg?
_____
_____

Reading
A magazine article

1 Before you read > Look at the picture and the title. What is the article about?

Akira, an amazing writer

The story of the smartphone novel

Some years ago, a 19-year-old Japanese girl began writing a novel about her life. She finished it in three weeks and she gave it the title *Dreams Come True*. Akira wasn't an experienced writer, but when a paper book version of her novel came out a few months later, a lot of people bought it. It was a great success and it sold over 200,000 copies. As a result, Akira became famous in her country.

It's an incredible story. But the most amazing thing about it is that Akira wrote the novel on her smartphone! She posted each chapter on a website and readers downloaded it immediately. They liked the story and they wanted to read more.

Did Akira enjoy writing her novel? Yes, she did. And when did she write it? She wrote it in her free time! Did she think much about the story? No, she didn't. And she didn't rewrite anything!

In Japan, there is a generation of young novelists. Akira is one of them. These young novelists write in simple, chatty style on their smartphones. They use abbreviations and emoticons. They use the same style that they use to write text messages and they don't worry too much about grammar and spelling.

At first, people were critical of these novels because they weren't "proper" literature. Today, they are very popular with people of all ages. Many of the best-selling paper books in Japan were originally smartphone novels.

2 Read for general ideas > Answer the questions.
1 Who is the author of *Dreams Come True*?

2 Was it about true experiences?

3 Was the book successful?

4 What is special about it?

3 Read for details > Circle the correct answers.
1 Akira wrote her novel very…
   a slowly. b quickly.

2 Akira … experience in writing books.
   a had b didn't have

3 People were first able to read *Dreams Come True*…
   a in paper books. b on the Internet.

4 Smartphone novelists write…
   a the way people speak. b in long sentences.

5 In Japan, smartphone novels are…
   a very successful. b only read by teenage girls.

COMPARING CULTURES
What do you think about smartphone novels? Do people read them in your country?

WEB QUEST

Find out about an amazing person.

1 Think of an amazing writer or choose a person from the quiz on page 43.
2 Find out more information about him/her.
3 Draw a timeline in your notebook and include important facts about his/her life.
4 Share the information with the class.

#tip

Find official websites or sites that contain biographies. To do your search, you can write: [person's name] biography.

Grammar
Simple past – regular and irregular verbs (2): questions

USE

A Analyze these sentences from the text on page 44. Underline seven more simple past verb forms.

She <u>gave</u> it the title *Dreams Come True*.
A lot of people bought it.
It sold over 200,000 copies.
She posted it on a website.
Readers downloaded it immediately.
They wanted to read more.
She wrote it in her free time.
She didn't rewrite anything.

B Analyze these questions and answers. Underline five more simple past forms.

<u>Did</u> Akira <u>enjoy</u> writing her novel?
Yes, she did.

When did she write it?
She wrote it in her free time.

Did she think much about the story?
No, she didn't.

FORM

C Classify the verbs from Activity A and from page 43. For each verb, write the infinitive form and the simple past form in your notebook.

regular verbs	irregular verbs
post – posted	give – gave

D Complete the chart.

Yes/No questions

| _____ | I / you / he / she / it / we / they | become | famous? |

Short answers

| Yes, | I / you / he / she / it / we / they | _____ . |
| No, | | didn't. |

Wh- questions

| When Where Why | _____ | I / you / he / she / we / they | write it? |

E Complete the diagrams with the simple past form of *buy*.

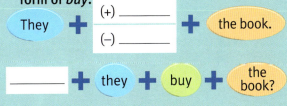

1 Complete the book review with the simple past form of the verbs in parentheses.

My brother (1) _____ (give) me *The Hunger Games* by Suzanne Collins for my last birthday. At first, I (2) _____ (not think) it was a good book, but when I (3) _____ (begin) reading it, I really (4) _____ (enjoy) it. I (5) _____ (not want) it to end!
I (6) _____ (think) the story was very original because it (7) _____ (have) a very unusual theme. I (8) _____ (like) the main character, Katniss Everdeen.

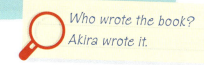

Who wrote the book?
Akira wrote it.

2 Order the words to make questions.

1 did / you / where / go / on vacation / ?
_____

2 do / what / you / yesterday / did / ?
_____

3 listen / when / you / did / music / to / ?
_____

3 Free practice > In turns, ask and answer the questions in Activity 2.

45

Build your skills

Reading & Listening
A festival web page

1 Before you read > Look at the web page. What is it about? Think of your age: can you go to TeenFest?

---

www.teenfestus.com

TEENFEST

ABOUT | **NEWS** | **BUY TICKETS** | **BANDS** | **PICTURES** | **FAQS** | **CONTACT US**

TeenFest is Greenville's first music festival exclusively organized for 13–17 year-olds*! For one day only, you can see loads of the most popular bands in one place.

Date: Saturday, March 19th 2016
Place: Green Park, Greenville
Time: 11:00 a.m.– 8:00 p.m.
Price: $15.00

Artists: Billy Jean, Two Dimensions, Dan May, The Hipsters, Yo-Yo, The Kinetics, and many more!

Food and drink available

* Strictly no entry for under 13s or over 17s. Picture ID is obligatory.

---

2 Read > Answer the questions.

1 When is the festival?

2 Where is it?

3 What time does it start?

4 What time does it finish?

5 How much are the tickets?

3 Give your opinion > Do you think this festival sounds fun? Why (not)? Discuss the matter with your classmates.

4 🔊 20 Listen to three announcements. In what order do you hear them? Write **1**, **2**, or **3**.

a Information about an African drumming class ☐
b An announcement about the end of the festival ☐
c Information about a Scottish pipe band ☐

5 🔊 20 Listen again. Circle the correct options.

1 The pipe band starts at **5 o'clock** / **7 o'clock**.
2 The drumming class is for **under 16s** / **adults**.
3 The festival closes in **ten** / **thirty** minutes.

Listening & Speaking
Talking about past events

1 Before you listen > Look at the picture of Hazel and James. Where are they? What are they doing?

_____
_____
_____

2 🔊 21 Listen for general ideas > Answer the questions.

1 What did James do last weekend?
_____

2 What did Hazel do?
_____

3 🔊 21 Listen for details > Complete the conversation.

Hi! Did you have a good (1) _____?	Yes, I did. It was (2) _____!
What did you (3) _____?	I went to a (4) _____ festival with my brother.
Really? How was it?	It was (5) _____! I saw some (6) _____ bands.
Wow! Cool.	Anyway, what about you? How was your weekend?
Oh, it was (7) _____.	What did you do?
Nothing (8) _____. I went shopping.	Oh, well. Next time you can come with us!

4 👤 Look at the tickets at the bottom of the page. Choose an event and imagine you went there last weekend. Invent answers to these questions.

1 What did you do last weekend?
_____

2 How was it?
_____

5 Speak > Role play in pairs.

1 Role play the conversation in Activity 3.
2 Role play a new conversation. Use information from the tickets.
3 Switch roles.

Keep it going!

Circle these words in the conversation.

Really?   Wow!

Remember to use them to show interest in what the other person is saying.

Writing
A review

1 Read Kate's review. Where was she last weekend? What did she like about it?

_____

_____

THE SHERLOCK HOLMES MUSEUM

My family and I are spending our summer vacation in Europe, and last weekend we went to The Sherlock Holmes Museum, in London. Sherlock Holmes is the main character of a series of detective stories by a Scottish author, Sir Arthur Conan Doyle.

The museum was small, but interesting. I looked around the different rooms. I saw lots of Sherlock Holmes's possessions, too. I also met characters from the books – but they were actors!

I enjoyed learning about Doyle. He wrote four novels and 56 short stories about Sherlock Holmes. He became famous because his stories were very good. He was born in 1859 and he died in 1930.

My favorite thing was the museum store. It had nice souvenirs and good books, and the prices were cheap. I bought a book about true detective stories.

I really enjoyed my visit to the museum. The only problem was that it was very busy. We waited for half an hour to buy our tickets.

Kate

3 Read the review again. <u>Underline</u> examples of sentences with *also* and *too*.

4 Rewrite the second sentences using the words in parentheses.

1 The stories were interesting. They were funny. (also)

_____

2 Young children liked it. Teenagers liked it. (too)

_____

3 The tickets were expensive. The café was expensive. (also)

_____

4 We enjoyed exploring the castle. We enjoyed exploring the gardens. (too)

_____

2 Read the "Write it right!" section.

Write it right!
Linkers

⇢ We use **also** and **too** to give more information about something.

⇢ We use **also** after *be* but before main verbs.

I visited the museum and I was also in the castle. I had lunch and I also bought souvenirs.

⇢ We use **too** at the end of sentences.

There's a store for visitors, too.

Writing task

Plan > Choose an interesting place you visited. Make notes in your notebook about:
- its name and location
- the things you did
- the things you liked / didn't like
- your favorite thing
- the things you bought

Write > Write your review. Remember to use:
- the simple past.
- *also* and *too* to give more information.

Check > Check your writing.

The Beat MAGAZINE

The Social Network

The Social Network (2010) is an American movie. It tells the story of Mark Zuckerberg, the creator of the Internet social networking site, Facebook.

The movie is directed by David Fincher. Actor Jesse Eisenberg plays Mark. What is Mark's story about?

Mark was a student at Harvard University, in the USA. He was a very intelligent student and he was brilliant with computers. He had a girlfriend, but he didn't have many friends and he wasn't very sociable. One day, his girlfriend left him. He was very angry with her and he wrote horrible things about her on his blog. Then he created a website, Facemash, and he invited boys at Harvard to write horrible things about the girls at the university. Facemash became popular and he started similar sites at other universities.

In time, he asked a friend, Eduardo Saverin, to lend him some money because he wanted to create another site. His friend gave him the money and he created Facebook. This new site became a big success, but soon problems started with his business partners and friends.

See the movie and tell us what you think about it.

---

1 🔊 22 Listen and read about the movie *The Social Network*. What is it about?
_____
_____

2 Read again and answer the questions.

1 What does the name of the movie refer to?
_____

2 Who is the main character in this movie?
_____

3 Which university did Mark go to?
_____

4 What kind of student was he?
_____
_____

5 Did he have any friends?
_____

6 What did he do when his girlfriend left him?
_____
_____

7 Why did he create Facemash?
_____
_____

8 What did he need to create Facebook?
_____

3 👤 Choose one of these activities.

1 Write five false sentences about the text on a slip of paper. Exchange slips with a classmate and correct the sentences.

2 Choose two facts about Mark's life. Explain why you agree / don't agree with what Mark did.

UNIT 4 Life on Earth

Vocabulary
Geographical features

1. Look at the article. Name the seven natural wonders.

2. 🔊 23 Listen and repeat the words in blue.

3. Match the seven wonders to the pictures.

WHAT ARE THE SEVEN NATURAL WONDERS OF THE WORLD?
Our readers chose these places!

1. Mount Everest, border of China and Nepal
You can go trekking to the base of this high mountain. Only experienced climbers can reach the top. It's 8,848 m high!

2. Victoria Falls, Africa
These impressive waterfalls are about 2 km wide and 100 m high. They are on the border of Zimbabwe and Zambia. In the dry season, you can walk across the top of the falls.

3. The Grand Canyon, USA
This amazing canyon is in the middle of a dry desert and it is nearly 2 km deep. You can go rafting down the Colorado River at the bottom of the valley.

4. The Amazon Rain forest, Brazil
This large rain forest is full of plants and animals. About 10% of the world's species live in this forest. You can travel by canoe down the Amazon River.

5. The Dead Sea, Jordan
The Dead Sea isn't a sea. It's a very big lake. Its water is salty and you can float on it! Its beach is very unusual. It doesn't have any white sand – it has a lot of brown mud.

6. The Blue Cave, Greece
On the Greek island of Kastelorizo, there is an interesting cave. Its water is a beautiful deep blue and you can visit it by boat.

7. The Great Barrier Reef, Australia
You can go snorkeling or diving in this huge coral reef in the Pacific Ocean. It has over 1,500 different kinds of fish. Some of them are very colorful.

4 Complete the chart with the words in blue from Activity 1.

Land	Water
mountain	waterfalls

5 Use the words from the box to label the pictures.

> float   go diving   go rafting
> go snorkeling   go trekking

1 _____

2 _____

3 _____

4 _____

5 _____

6 Complete the sentences about things you can do at the natural wonders.

You can…

1 _____ to the base of Mount Everest.
2 _____ the top of Victoria Falls in the dry season.
3 _____ down the Colorado River.
4 _____ down the Amazon River.
5 _____ on the salty water of the Dead Sea.
6 _____ the Blue Cave _____.
7 _____ or _____ in the Great Barrier Reef.

7 Find the adjectives below in the text. What do they describe?

1 high _____
2 impressive _____
3 amazing _____
4 dry _____
5 large _____
6 salty _____
7 unusual _____
8 interesting _____
9 huge _____
10 colorful _____

8 In turns, talk about the natural wonders you'd like to visit. Say what you can do there.

🟠 I'd like to go to Mount Everest because it's amazing. You can go trekking to its base.
🔵 Me too. And I also want to…

LEARNING TO LEARN

To practice new words, read a piece of information and write a sentence about it. Then compare it with the piece you read.

Mount Everest is a high mountain in China and Nepal.

Reading
A web article

1 Before you read > Look at the picture, title, and subtitle of the article. What is it about?

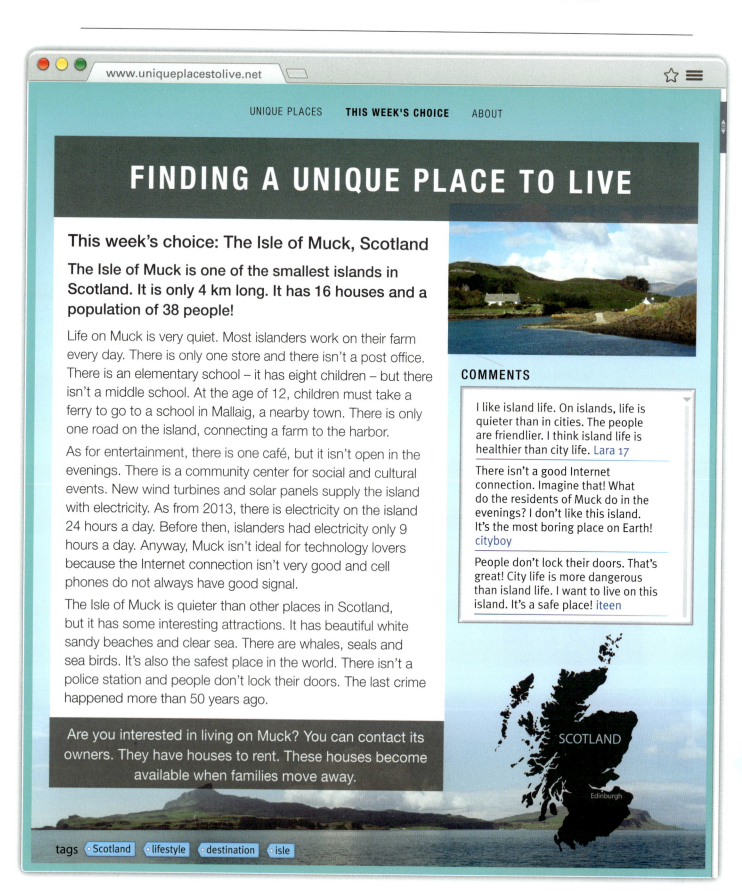

FINDING A UNIQUE PLACE TO LIVE

This week's choice: The Isle of Muck, Scotland

The Isle of Muck is one of the smallest islands in Scotland. It is only 4 km long. It has 16 houses and a population of 38 people!

Life on Muck is very quiet. Most islanders work on their farm every day. There is only one store and there isn't a post office. There is an elementary school – it has eight children – but there isn't a middle school. At the age of 12, children must take a ferry to go to a school in Mallaig, a nearby town. There is only one road on the island, connecting a farm to the harbor.

As for entertainment, there is one café, but it isn't open in the evenings. There is a community center for social and cultural events. New wind turbines and solar panels supply the island with electricity. As from 2013, there is electricity on the island 24 hours a day. Before then, islanders had electricity only 9 hours a day. Anyway, Muck isn't ideal for technology lovers because the Internet connection isn't very good and cell phones do not always have good signal.

The Isle of Muck is quieter than other places in Scotland, but it has some interesting attractions. It has beautiful white sandy beaches and clear sea. There are whales, seals and sea birds. It's also the safest place in the world. There isn't a police station and people don't lock their doors. The last crime happened more than 50 years ago.

Are you interested in living on Muck? You can contact its owners. They have houses to rent. These houses become available when families move away.

COMMENTS

I like island life. On islands, life is quieter than in cities. The people are friendlier. I think island life is healthier than city life. Lara 17

There isn't a good Internet connection. Imagine that! What do the residents of Muck do in the evenings? I don't like this island. It's the most boring place on Earth! cityboy

People don't lock their doors. That's great! City life is more dangerous than island life. I want to live on this island. It's a safe place! iteen

tags: Scotland, lifestyle, destination, isle

2 Read for general ideas > Answer the questions.

1 Where is Muck?
___
2 How many people live on the island?
___
3 Is life quiet or busy on Muck?
___
4 Is it a dangerous place?
___
5 Does cityboy like the island? Why (not)?
___
6 Does iteen like it? Why (not)?
___

3 Read for details > Circle *T* (true) or *F* (false). Correct the false statements with excerpts from the article.

1 The Isle of Muck is 16 km long.   T F
___
2 There is a farm on the island.   T F
___
3 Teens who are 14 years old can't study on the island.   T F
___
4 You can drink coffee at the café at 8 p.m.   T F
___
5 In 2010, people could charge their cell phones all day long.   T F
___
6 The beaches on the Isle of Muck are clean.   T F
___

7 People can see different sea animals on the island.   T F
___
8 A thief robbed a tourist on the island in 2013.   T F
___

4 Read for details > What is there on the Isle of Muck? Check (✓) the correct options.

a large population ☐
a farm ☐
a store ☐
a post office ☐
an elementary school ☐
a middle school ☐
an evening café ☐
electricity ☐
a good Internet connection ☐
good cell phone signal ☐
sandy beaches ☐
a police station ☐
a lot of crimes ☐
a community center ☐

5 Read for inference > Circle the comments that refer to the web article.

> I love to visit big cities! They're much more interesting than small towns. And I also like places with lots of people – it's a great way to make new friends! CrowdGirl
>
> In my opinion, islands are fantastic places. The nature, animals, and views are unique. I'll talk to my parents about visiting this island on our next vacation! Lukas2005
>
> Scotland is a fascinating country. I visited Edinburgh and Glasgow last year, but I didn't visit these islands. I don't know If I'd like to go there, because I can't live without an Internet connection. MobileJack
>
> This small island in Africa is just amazing! I love the rain forest and tropical islands. There is a very nice hotel there – it is the most comfortable place on the island. Mel 14

COMPARING CULTURES

Are there any islands in your country? Do people live on them? Name places of high and low population density.

WEB QUEST

Find out information about an island in your country.

1 In pairs, choose an island in your country you would like to learn about.
2 Make notes about its climate, population, history, typical food and getting to the island.
3 Share the information with the class.

#tip

To do your search, you can write on the search engine: [*name of the island*] climate or any other information you want to find out about the place.

Grammar
Adjectives: comparative and superlative forms

USE

A Analyze these sentences from the text on page 52. Underline two more comparative forms.

The Isle of Muck is quieter than other places in Scotland.

Island life is healthier than city life.

City life is more dangerous than island life.

B Analyze these sentences from the text on page 52. Underline two more superlative forms.

The Isle of Muck is one of the smallest islands in Scotland.

It's also the safest place in the world.

It's the most boring place on Earth.

C Circle the correct option to complete the rules.

We use the comparative form to compare **two / three or more** people or things.

We use the superlative form to compare **two / three or more** people or things.

FORM

D Complete the chart.

Adjective	Comparative	Superlative
quiet		the quietest
healthy		the healthiest
small	smaller	
safe	safer	
dangerous		the most dangerous
boring	more boring	

E Complete the diagrams.

One-syllable adjectives or two-syllable adjectives ending in -y:

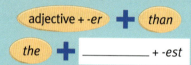

Most adjectives of two or more syllables:

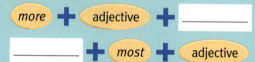

F Look at the chart. Are *good* and *bad* regular or irregular adjectives? Why? Answer orally.

Adjective	Comparative	Superlative
good	better	the best
bad	worse	the worst

---

1 Complete the sentences with the comparative or superlative form of the adjectives in parentheses.

1 The Amazon rain forest has _____ collection of plants and animals in the world. (large)
2 Mount Everest is _____ mountain in the world. (high)
3 The Nile River in Egypt is _____ river in the world. (long)
4 The Victoria Falls are _____ the Niagara Falls. (large)

2 Complete the questions with the superlative form of the adjectives in parentheses. Then answer about your country.

Which is...
1 _____ (high) mountain?
2 _____ (long) river?
3 _____ (big) lake?
4 _____ (beautiful) beach?

COMPARING LANGUAGES

In English, we can add -er or -est to form comparative and superlative adjectives. How do you make comparisons in your language?

Vocabulary
Environmental issues

1 🔊 24 Listen and repeat the sentences in the boxes. Are any of these things happening in your country? If so, where? Discuss with your classmates.

People are...		Animals are...	Ice platforms are...
cutting down trees.	leaving trash on beaches.	dying.	melting.
disturbing animals.	building new houses and roads.	losing their habitat.	
hunting animals.			

2 Read the article. Complete the text with the verbs from Activity 1. Use one of the verbs twice.

www.environmentalfans.com

NATURE FANS — NEWS VIDEOS PICTURES ENVIRONMENT

10 ENDANGERED SPECIES *These animals are in danger of extinction. Read and find out!*

The climate is changing. Summers are hotter and winters are colder than in the past. Monarch butterflies are (1) _____. Mountain gorillas live in forests. They are (2) _____ their habitat because people are (3) _____ trees. Polar bears and penguins can't find enough food because ice platforms are (4) _____. Polar bears hunt seals from ice platforms. Penguins eat fish and fish feed on organisms that grow on ice. Tourists are (5) _____ trash on beaches and (6) _____ sea turtles. These animals need to lay their eggs on clean beaches. Poachers are illegal hunters. They are (7) _____ tigers for their fur, rhinos for their horns and elephants for their tusks. Cities are growing. Crocodiles are (8) _____ their habitat because people are (9) _____ new houses and roads.

3 Answer the questions.

1 Why are monarch butterflies dying?
_____

2 Why are gorillas and crocodiles losing their habitat?
_____
_____

3 Why can't penguins and polar bears find enough food?
_____

4 Why do poachers hunt tigers, rhinos, and elephants?
_____
_____

4 👤 What other endangered animals do you know? Why are they in danger? Discuss with your classmates.

Listening
Endangered animals

5 🔊 25 Listen to Chris and Lucy talking about a school project. What mistake does Chris make?
_____

6 🔊 25 Listen again. Underline the correct words to complete the sentences.

1 Lucy chooses **snakes / whales** for her project.

2 Whales are very intelligent because they can **communicate with / hunt** other whales.

3 Whales are very friendly because they **play with people / swim near boats**.

4 Ships are dangerous to whales because they **hit and kill / disturb** whales.

Reading
An online travel guide

1 Before you read > Look at the pictures. What can you see?

___

Travelers Favorite Guide

Destinations | Hotels | Tips | What tourists say

Interview with Sabrina Walkers, guest at THULA THULA WILDLIFE RESERVE in South Africa

HOW MANY ANIMALS ARE THERE IN THE RESERVE?
I don't know exactly, but there are a lot of animals, including rhinos, elephants, leopards, crocodiles, and giraffes. There aren't any lions or cheetahs.

IS THERE A HOTEL?
Yes, there is. Guests can stay in comfortable tents or beautiful rooms. All the rooms have a veranda with a view of the African bush.

ARE THERE ANY RESTAURANTS?
Yes, there is a good restaurant. You can try some traditional food. The African "braai" (barbecue) is delicious!

WHAT CAN GUESTS DO?
There are a lot of things to do. Local guides take tourists on safaris. They also take them on walks to learn about unusual plants in the area.

DID YOU SEE ANY WILDLIFE ON YOUR SAFARI?
Yes, I did! I saw a lot of animals and I had a lot of fun.

DO THEY PROTECT ANIMALS AT THULA THULA?
Yes, they do. But there aren't many endangered animals at the reserve. In October 2009, the reserve adopted two baby rhinos, Thabo and Ntombi. Today, they live in the wild, but they can't be on their own. Armed guards must accompany them 24 hours a day to protect them against poachers.

IS THERE ANY ILLEGAL HUNTING IN THE RESERVE?
Yes, sadly, there is. There are a lot of illegal hunters in the area. In August 2009, some poachers killed Heidi, a female white rhino from the reserve.

WHEN IS THE BEST TIME TO GO?
The reserve is open all year round. Summers are hot and winters are warm. There isn't much rain in South Africa and there are a lot of sunny days.

HOW CAN GUESTS GET THERE?
There is an airport only 45 minutes away.

HOW MUCH MONEY DID YOU SPEND ON YOUR TRIP?
A lot! The reserve is an expensive place, but it's amazing!

tags | South Africa | reserve | exotic destinations

2 Read for general ideas > Answer the questions.
1. What is Thula Thula?
2. What animals live there?
3. What can guests do?
4. Do they protect animals at Thula Thula?

3 Read for details > Complete the sentences.
1. At Thula Thula, guests stay at _____.
2. They can eat _____.
3. Thabo and Ntombi are _____.
4. Thabo and Ntombi can't be alone because of _____.
5. Heidi was _____.
6. You can visit Thula Thula _____.
7. The hottest time of the year is _____.

Grammar
a / an, some, any, not much / many, a lot of, How much / many...?

USE

A Analyze these sentences from the text on page 56. Pay attention to the words in bold. Write *C* (Countable) or *U* (Uncountable).

How many **animals** are there? ☐
There aren't any **lions**. ☐
Is there a **hotel** in the reserve? ☐
You can try some traditional **food**. ☐
There are a lot of **things** to do. ☐
Did you see any **wildlife** on your safari? ☐
I had a lot of **fun**. ☐
I didn't have any **time** to go on one. ☐
Are there any **restaurants**? ☐
Is there any illegal **hunting**? ☐
Some **poachers** killed Heidi. ☐
There isn't much **rain**. ☐
How much **money** did you spend on your trip? ☐
There is an **airport** near the reserve. ☐

FORM

B Complete the charts with examples.

singular countable nouns
a hotel   **an** _____

	plural countable nouns	uncountable nouns
Affirmative	**some** poachers **a lot of** _____	**some** _____ **a lot of** fun
Negative	**any** _____ **many** _____	**any** time **much** _____
Yes/No questions	Are there **any** _____?	Is there **any** illegal hunting?
Questions	How many _____?	How much _____?

C Complete the chart with the words in bold in Activity A.

countable nouns	uncountable nouns
animals	food

1 Complete the sentences with *a / an*, *some* or *any*.

1 That's _____ elephant!
2 The reserve is home to _____ rescued animals.
3 I don't have _____ camera.
4 There aren't _____ rhinos on the island.
5 Are there _____ cheap rooms in this hotel?
6 I ate _____ traditional food.
7 Is there _____ clean water in the reserve?

2 Look at the picture. Then correct the sentences. Use *a lot of*, *many*, and *much*.

1 She doesn't have much sunscreen.
   _____
2 She has a lot of mosquito bites.
   _____
3 There's a lot of space in the room.
   _____
4 There aren't any mosquitoes.
   _____

3 🗣 Free practice > Choose a picture from a magazine. Then in turns, ask and answer about it.

🟠 *Are there any people?*
🔵 *Yes, there are.*
🟠 *How many people are there?*
🔵 *There are three people.*

Build your skills

Reading & Listening
An NGO leaflet

1 Before you read > Look at the leaflet. What is it about?

_____

HAVE FUN AND DO SOMETHING USEFUL THIS WEEKEND!

Are you aged 14-16? We need you for these great volunteer days!

WORK WITH WILDLIFE ☐
Work in a zoo and help the zookeepers for a day. You can feed the animals or clean the penguin pool. More activities available!
Location: Springfield Zoo

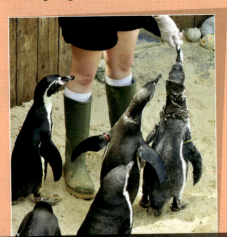

CLEAN A BEACH ☐
Join one of our "green" teams at your local beach on Saturday and help to pick up trash.
Location: all over the country

BE A FRIEND TO A BLIND TEENAGER ☐
Accompany a blind teenager on vacation in New York and help him or her "see" the sights through your eyes.
Location: New York

HELP SOME INSECTS ☐
Bees and butterflies are disappearing from the countryside. Plant flowers to help to bring them back.
Location: Green Valley National Park

🔍 Visit www.volunteerdays.com to find out more about volunteer work in your area.

2 Read > Answer the questions.

In which activity or activities can you...
1 help another person?
_____
2 do something positive for the environment?
_____
3 care for animals?
_____

3 👤 Give your opinion > Which activity sounds the most interesting? Why? Share your ideas with your classmates.

4 🔊 26 Listen to three short conversations. Check (✓) the activities from the leaflet the teenagers are doing.

5 🔊 26 Listen again and answer the questions in your notebook.

Conversation 1
1 What does the boy want to do?
2 What does he see?

Conversation 2
3 Where are the boy and the girl?
4 Where are they going?

Conversation 3
5 What food is the boy giving the giraffes?
6 Where are the people going next?

Listening & Speaking
Expressing preferences

1 **Before you listen** > Look at the picture. Where are the people in the picture? Who is interested in a volunteer day?

_____

_____

2 🔊 27 **Listen for general ideas** > Check (✓) the activities Lucy wants to do.

1 Work in the gift store. ☐
2 Help wildlife and work with animals. ☐
3 Clean the penguin pool. ☐
4 Help a zookeeper to feed the animals. ☐

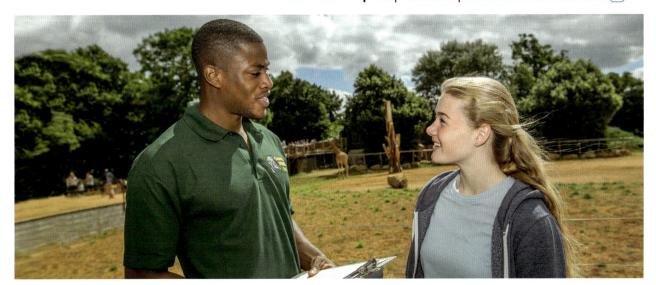

3 🔊 27 **Listen for details** > Complete the conversation.

Hello there, how can I (1) _____ ?	Hello, I'd like to sign up for the (2) _____ day.
Great! Do you want to (3) _____ in the zoo gift store?	That's a (4) _____ idea, but I want to help wildlife. I'd rather do something with the (5) _____ .
OK. How about cleaning the (6) _____ pool?	Well, _____ , but I don't really like (7) _____ ! Could I feed the animals?
Yes, maybe that's a (8) _____ idea for you. You can help one of the zookeepers (9) _____ the elephants.	Thanks! That sounds more (10) _____ than the other activities.
No problem!	Do you need (11) _____ details from me?
Yes, could you please fill in this (12) _____ ?	OK!

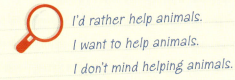

I'd rather help animals.
I want to help animals.
I don't mind helping animals.

4 **Speak** > Role play in pairs.

1 Role play the conversation in Activity 3.
2 Role play a new conversation. Use information from the leaflet on page 58.
3 Switch roles.

Keep it going!

Underline these phrases in the conversation.

I'd like to…   I want to…   I'd rather…
Could I… ?   I don't mind… but I don't really like…

Remember to use them to express your preferences.

Writing
A travel guide article

1 Read the travel guide article. What country is it about? What can you do there?

All you want to know about Greece!

How many tourists visit Greece every year?
A lot of tourists visit this country because it has nice weather, beautiful scenery and friendly people.

When is the best time of the year to visit Greece?
Greece has long summers and short winters. July and August are the hottest months of the year, but temperatures are warm from May to October. There isn't much rain in the summer.

What can you do in Greece?
You can visit impressive ancient monuments in Athens or relax on the country's beautiful small islands. Greece has some of the most beautiful islands in the world.

How many islands are there in Greece?
There are hundreds! They have white sandy beaches and clear blue sea.

Is there any wildlife in Greece?
Yes, there is. A lot of people don't know that Greece has many forests and mountains with a lot of wildlife. There are buffalos, bears, and butterflies in its national parks. There are a lot of turtles, seals, and dolphins near the islands.

Are there any good restaurants?
Yes, there are! And you can eat traditional food. In Greece, you must try some delicious fresh fish.

EUROPE

2 Read the "Write it right!" section.

Write it right!
Order of adjectives

⇢ When we use two or more adjectives together, we use the following order:
opinion size age shape color origin material + noun

They have white sandy beaches.
(color) (material)

You must try some delicious fresh fish.
(opinion) (age)

3 Classify the adjectives in the chart.

> large   quiet   beautiful   fresh   rocky
> amazing   blue   old   modern   salty   white
> interesting   small   impressive   big
> sandy   high   colorful   new   delicious
> unusual   dangerous   ancient

Writing task

Plan > Choose a country or a natural wonder. In your notebook, write 6–8 interesting questions and then answer them.

Write > Write your article. Remember to use:
- vocabulary on geographical features and animals.
- *a/an, some, any, a lot of, not much/many, How much/many...?*
- adjectives + nouns.

Check > Check your writing.

Opinion	
Size	
Age	
Color	
Material	

The Beat MAGAZINE

Beach Park volunteer work team

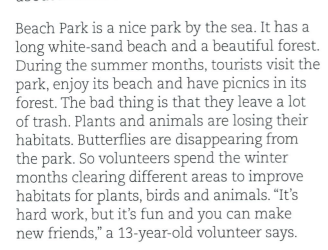

Do you care about animals and their habitats? Are you worried about the environment? Then this is your chance to do something about it! Read this article and find out how you can help.

Beach Park is a nice park by the sea. It has a long white-sand beach and a beautiful forest. During the summer months, tourists visit the park, enjoy its beach and have picnics in its forest. The bad thing is that they leave a lot of trash. Plants and animals are losing their habitats. Butterflies are disappearing from the park. So volunteers spend the winter months clearing different areas to improve habitats for plants, birds and animals. "It's hard work, but it's fun and you can make new friends," a 13-year-old volunteer says.

Everyone is welcome to do conservation work from October to March and you don't need to have any previous experience. You just need to be ready to help! The park's staff provides all the tools and training for each task. They also serve water, coffee and cookies, but you have to take a packed lunch. It is important that you wear jeans and boots. Comfortable clothes are essential for this type of work.

If you are ready to become a volunteer and you want to do something different this winter, please contact the park's warden, Ian Jones, on 555-6874, so that he can give you all the details to get started!

Read Amy's story and get inspired!

I worked as a volunteer for the first time last year and I really enjoyed it. We picked up a lot of trash and we also planted flowers. This year, a lot of butterflies are coming back to the park. Last week, I talked to the warden and he told me the plans for this winter: clean the beach and build a picnic area. I think it's a great idea. Come and help us to save our park!

---

1 🔊 28 **Listen and read about volunteer work. What is Beach Park volunteer work about?**

_____

_____

2 Read again and answer the questions.

1 What is there at Beach Park?

_____

2 When do tourists go to the park?

_____

3 When do volunteers work at the park?

_____

4 Why is their work important?

_____

_____

5 What do volunteers need to take?

_____

3 👤 **Choose one of these activities.**

1 In your notebook, write a paragraph explaining why you want to be a volunteer at Beach Park.
2 Write five false sentences about the text on a slip of paper. Exchange slips with a classmate and correct the sentences.

UNIT 3 PROGRESS CHECK

Vocabulary

Types of books

1 Write words for types of books.

1 A story about life in the future: _____
2 A story that makes you laugh: _____
3 A person's life in his/her own words: _____
4 A story that is full of danger and suspense: _____

⬜ / 4 points

Verbs to talk about people's lives in the past

2 Complete the sentences with the simple past form of the verbs from the box.

> buy found earn think
> win sell give create

1 Mandela _____ discrimination was wrong.
2 Malala Yousafzai _____ the Nobel Peace Prize in 2014.
3 J.K. Rowling _____ millions of copies of the *Harry Potter* books.
4 Steve Jobs _____ Apple in the United States.
5 Yesterday, I _____ tickets for a concert.
6 My sister _____ me a nice gift for my birthday!
7 Mark Zuckerberg _____ Facebook and _____ a lot of money.

⬜ / 8 points

Grammar

Be – simple past

3 Complete the statements and questions with the simple past form of *be*.

1 The travel guide _____ (not) useful.
2 The books _____ very expensive.
3 Where _____ you yesterday?

⬜ / 3 points

Simple past – regular and irregular verbs (2)

4 Complete the questions with the simple past form of the verbs in parentheses.

1 _____ (he / download) music from the Internet yesterday?
2 _____ (she / post) any new comments last week?
3 _____ (you / go) to the movies last Friday?

⬜ / 3 points

5 Complete the interview with the simple past form of the verbs in parentheses.

Who (1) _____ (be) Charles Dickens?
He (2) _____ (be) an English writer. He (3) _____ (live) from 1812 to 1870. He (4) _____ (write) 15 novels, including *A Christmas Carol* and *Oliver Twist*.

What (5) _____ (he / write) about?
A lot of his books (6) _____ (be) about poor people. They (7) _____ (not have) an easy life in the 19th century and Dickens (8) _____ (think) this was wrong. He (9) _____ (want) to make people think about these problems.

Why (10) _____ (people / like) his books?
Because they (11) _____ (have) exciting stories and interesting characters. Everyone (12) _____ (like) them at his time!

⬜ / 12 points

Total Score: ⬜ / 30 points

Check your performance!

Try again! 0–9 Keep up! 10–16 Well done! 17–23 Great job! 24–30

Vocabulary
Geographical features

1 Look at the pictures and complete the sentences.

1 We saw some beautiful _____.
2 We went trekking to an impressive _____.

3 We crossed a very dry _____.
4 We took pictures of a green _____.

5 We took a boat to a large _____.
6 We climbed a very high _____.

☐ / 6 points

Environmental issues

2 Complete the verbs.

1 Whales are in danger because some people are still h_____ them.
2 Monarch butterflies are d_____ because the climate is changing.
3 Polar bears can't find food because the Arctic ice is m_____.
4 Some gorillas can't find a place to live because people are cutting d_____ trees.
5 Tourists are disturbing sea turtles. They are l_____ trash on the beach.
6 Crocodiles are in danger because they are l_____ their habitat.

☐ / 6 points

Grammar
Adjectives: comparative and superlative forms

3 Complete the sentences with the comparative or superlative form of the adjectives in parentheses.

1 The crocodile is one of _____ animals on Earth. (old)
2 In my country, winters are _____ summers. (bad)
3 Lions are _____ elephants. (dangerous)
4 Thula Thula is one of _____ reserves in Africa. (expensive)
5 The Pacific Ocean is _____ the Caribbean Sea. (cold)

☐ / 5 points

a / an, some, any, not much / many, a lot of, How much / many...?

4 Complete the sentences.

1 I'd like _____ information, please. Is there _____ airport near the reserve?
2 How _____ time do we have? I want to take a picture of _____ elephant.
3 Is there _____ illegal hunting in this area? I can see _____ armed men near those trees!
4 I didn't see _____ wildlife. Did you see _____ animals?
5 Is this _____ reserve? How _____ endangered species live here?

☐ / 10 points

5 Look at the picture and complete the sentences with *much*, *many*, or *a lot of*.

1 There are _____ trees.
2 There are _____ elephants.
3 There isn't _____ water.

☐ / 3 points

Check your performance!

Total Score: ☐ / 30 points

PROGRESS CHECK

UNIT 4

UNIT 5 Special days

Vocabulary
Celebrations

1 🔊 29 Listen and repeat the phrases in the box. Which things do you do for someone's birthday? Circle them.

> eat special food   visit relatives   watch street parades   send cards
> give presents   have a party   go to church   get together
> decorate the house   light a bonfire   sing songs
> celebrate an anniversary   watch fireworks   wear a costume   have fun

2 Read the article. Where are these girls from? Complete the text with verbs from Activity 1.

Special days around the world

July 4th – Independence Day

On Independence Day, we often (1) _____ the house in red, white, and blue because they are the colors of our flag. We (2) _____ a party at home and we (3) _____ special songs. We don't (4) _____ costumes, but we often wear red, white and blue clothes or a flag pin. We (5) _____ street parades in the afternoon.

November 5th – Bonfire Night

December 25th– Christmas

Here, Christmas is in the summer vacation – it's often hot, about 30 °C! We always decorate a Christmas tree, (6) _____ cards, and (7) _____ presents. Some people (8) _____ to church. On Christmas Eve – December 24th – we usually (9) _____ relatives and (10) _____ special food. We (11) _____ fireworks at midnight to celebrate the start of Christmas Day. Then we (12) _____ fun opening presents. We usually go to bed very late!

On November 5th, we (13) _____ the anniversary of the Gunpowder Plot – an attempt to blow up the Houses of Parliament in London and kill the king, that happened in the 17th century! On Bonfire Night we (14) _____ a bonfire and (15) _____ fireworks. People burn a homemade model of a man in the fire – he symbolizes Guy Fawkes, the leader of the plot. Family and friends also (16) _____ together to celebrate and (17) _____ special food.

3 Look at other activities people do on special days. Use the phrases in the box to label the pictures.

> dance to traditional music   go out for dinner   play party games   sing "Happy Birthday"

4 What special days do you celebrate? When do you celebrate them? Complete the chart.

Special day	Date

5 In pairs, share the special days in Activity 4. Say when you celebrate them.

🟠 *We celebrate Spring Day on September 21st.*

6 In pairs, ask and answer about your celebrations from Activities 4 and 5. Use words from Activities 1 and 3.

🟠 *How do you usually celebrate your birthday?*
🔵 *I usually have a party and...*

People celebrate Christmas on December 25th.
We celebrate Mother's Day on the second Sunday in May.

LEARNING TO LEARN
To practice verbs + nouns, make a list in your notebook of verbs and write nouns you can use with them.

watch + street parades, fireworks, TV,...

Reading
Blog entries

1 Before you read > Look at the blog quickly. What is the name of the boy? What is he celebrating?

---

www.my13adventures.blogginglife.com

13 adventures for my 13th year!

▶ June (2)
▼ July (1)
    About me
View my profile
Photo album

My 13 adventures

1. Visit New York
2. Watch a Knicks' game
3. Try 13 new sports
4. Go camping
5. Join a band
6. Run a 5K race
7. Learn Spanish
8. Read 13 books
9. Learn to juggle
10. Learn to cook
11. Travel by plane
12. Do volunteer work
13. Adopt a dog!

June 22nd
Next Saturday I'm going to be 13…

… and I'm going to have a big party! After that, it's going to be a special year. I'm going to have 13 new adventures (click on the links to see more about them). Enjoy my blog and please send me your comments!

Posted by Hazel at 8:32 p.m.
Great idea, James – I love your list of adventures! Your blog looks great and I can't wait to read it. When are you going to travel to New York? Are you going to post pictures of your trip?

June 25th
Tomorrow's the big day!

My older brother's decorating the house – he's going to fill it with balloons and I'm going to help him. My sister's going to make an enormous chocolate cake. 🙂

Posted by Aunt Anne at 5:12 p.m.
Happy birthday, James! Have a great day. Sorry, we can't come to your party. ☹ Uncle Bill sends his greetings! What time is your flight going to arrive here in New York on July 2nd?

July 1st
It's official: I'm a teenager!

The party was fantastic! I want to thank you all for the amazing presents. Now my year of adventures begins… with a trip to New York! My aunt lives there and I'm going to visit her. She's going to take me to watch the New York Knicks play at the Madison Square Garden!

Posted by John at 10:52 p.m.
Congratulations on officially becoming a teenager! Have fun in New York. What are you going to do for your next adventure?

2 Read for general ideas > Answer the questions.

1 When is James's birthday?
_____

2 What are his plans for his birthday?
_____
_____

3 Who posts comments on his blog?
_____

4 How many adventures are there on his list?
_____

3 Read for details > Circle *T* (True) or *F* (False).

1 James created a blog about his birthday. T F
2 Hazel wants to read James's blog. T F
3 On June 25th, James and his brother filled the house with balloons. T F
4 James liked his presents. T F
5 James lives in New York. T F

4 Read for details > Find the information below.

1 A person who really likes James's blog: _____

2 The person responsible for the cake at James's party: _____

3 Two relatives who are not going to go to James's party: _____

4 The date James is going to arrive in New York: _____

5 An adventure from James's list that he has on July 2nd: _____

6 The sport the New York Knicks play: _____

5 Read for inference > Which of his 13 adventures is James talking about? Complete the blog entries.

August 4th
The audition

As I mentioned before, one of my 13 adventures this year is to (1) _____. I'm going to participate in an audition at school today. I practiced a lot for it – I played the guitar so hard that my fingers hurt! Wish me luck!

August 27th
Chef James

Now to the next adventure: (2) _____!
Aunt Anne gave me a voucher for classes on my birthday. I'm going to have my first class at a local cooking school tomorrow. According to the program, we're going to make cupcakes!

September 25th
Run, James, run!

I'm going to (3) _____ next month. In order to be ready, I go jogging at the park every evening with Mia, my best friend. She's great at that! In the sports event, we're going to help a charity raise funds to help girls attend school in developing countries.

November 13th
Buddy's in the house

As part of my 13 adventures, I said that I wanted to (4) _____, remember? Well, my sister and I went to a shelter yesterday and met a lovely puppy – and we brought it home! His name's Buddy and he's a lot of fun! We're going to take him to the vet tomorrow to check if everything's OK with him.

December 1st
The first novel...

I'm kind of late with this adventure, but I'll try to (5) _____ in one year. The first on my list was *Harry Potter and the Philosopher's Stone* - yeah, that's right, this was my first HP book. The story is amazing! JK Rowling is an incredible writer. I'm sure the all that other books in the saga will be on my list.

6 In pairs, talk about James's 13 adventures. Which activity would you also like to do? Why?

🟠 *I'd like to learn Spanish because I like the language.*
🔵 *And I'd like to do volunteer work because I like to help people.*

COMPARING CULTURES

How do your friends celebrate their birthday? How do you usually celebrate your birthday?

67

Grammar
Going to: affirmative, negative, and questions
Object pronouns

USE

A Analyze these sentences from the text on page 66. Underline five more examples of *going to*.

I'm going to have a big party.

It's going to be a special year.

When are you going to travel to New York?

Are you going to post pictures of your trip?

He's going to fill it with balloons.

What are you going to do for your next adventure?

B Answer the questions.

What do we use *going to* for?

_____

C Analyze these sentences. Match the object pronouns to the words they refer to.

1 Click on the links to see more about <u>them</u>. ☐
2 Please send <u>me</u> your comments. ☐
3 I can't wait to read <u>it</u>. ☐
4 I'm going to help <u>him</u>. ☐
5 I want to thank <u>you</u> all for the presents. ☐
6 I'm going to visit <u>her</u>. ☐

a James	**d** his adventures
b his aunt	**e** his blog
c his friends	**f** his brother

FORM

D Look at Activity A and complete the chart.

Affirmative and negative

I	_____ / 'm not	going to	go.
He / She / It	_____ / isn't		
We / You / They	're / aren't		

Yes/No questions

Am	I	going _____	have fun?
Is	he / she / it		
_____	we / you / they		

Short answers

Yes, / No,	I	am. / 'm not.
	he / she / it	_____. / isn't.
	we / you / they	are. / _____.

Wh- questions

What When Where How	**is**	he / she / it	_____	play?
	are	we / you / they	to	

E Look at Activity C and complete the chart.

Subject pronouns

I	you	he	she	it	we	they

Object pronouns

_____	_____	_____	_____	it	us	_____

F Complete the rules with *subject* and *object*.

We use _____ pronouns + verbs.

We use verbs or prepositions + _____ pronouns.

---

1 Complete the conversation with the affirmative, negative, or question form of *going to*.

Ben: How (1) _____ (you / celebrate) your birthday?

(2) _____ (you / have) a party?

Ann: No, I (3) _____ (have) dinner with friends.

Ben: Really? What (4) _____ (you / cook)?

Ann: I (5) _____ (not cook)!

We (6) _____ (have) dinner in a restaurant.

2 Complete the sentences with object pronouns.

1 I love street parades. I always watch _____.
2 Our English teacher always gives _____ homework.
3 It's Sarah's birthday! Are you going to give _____ a present?

68

Vocabulary
Adverbs of manner

1 🔊 30 Look at the quiz. What is it about? Listen and repeat the words in blue.

_____

2 👤 Do the quiz. What's your score?

_____

3 Look at the quiz again and complete the chart.

Adjective	Adverb
quick	
hard	
loud	
nice	
healthy	
regular	
good	
easy	
dangerous	
happy	
bad	

Listening
Resolutions

4 🔊 31 Listen to an extract from the news. Answer the questions.

1 Where is the reporter?

_____

2 What day is it?

_____

3 What are the people waiting for?

_____
_____

5 🔊 31 Listen again. Complete the resolutions.
1 The first woman is going to learn _____.
2 The man is going to exercise _____.
3 The second woman is going to eat _____ and be _____.
4 The teen boy is going to study _____ and pass _____.
5 The second man is going to be _____ and have more _____.

Do you have good intentions?

Today is a good day to reconsider your resolutions for the year!

1 School
What's your attitude towards school this year?
a) Maximum results with minimum effort. I'm going to do my homework as quickly as possible so I can go out with my friends!
b) I'm going to work hard and practice my English every day.

2 Home and family
Are you an angel or a little devil at home? Choose your resolution:
a) My room is my space... I'm going to play my music as loudly as I want!
b) I promise to clean my room and speak nicely to my family.

3 Health and fitness
Are you planning to be healthier this year?
a) No way! My health routine starts next year...
b) Yes – I'm going to eat healthily, relax more and exercise regularly.

4 Friends
Are you a good friend?
a) Who needs real friends? I have hundreds on Facebook.
b) Friends are precious! I'm going to treat my old friends well and make new friends more easily.

5 The year ahead
What's your motto for the year ahead?
a) Live dangerously – you're young only once!
b) Live happily – that's the most important thing!

Points: a) = 2   b) = 3

Your score:
10–12 What a disaster! Do you really want to behave so badly this year?

13–15 Great! You have so many good intentions. You're going to do very well this year!

Reading
Posts on a travel website

1 Before you read > Read the title and look at the pictures. What is the website about? Where are the pictures from?

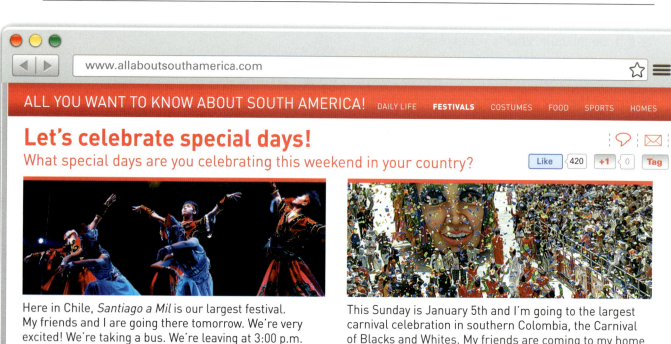

www.allaboutsouthamerica.com

ALL YOU WANT TO KNOW ABOUT SOUTH AMERICA!   DAILY LIFE   **FESTIVALS**   COSTUMES   FOOD   SPORTS   HOMES

Let's celebrate special days!
What special days are you celebrating this weekend in your country?

Like | 420 | +1 | 0 | Tag

Here in Chile, *Santiago a Mil* is our largest festival. My friends and I are going there tomorrow. We're very excited! We're taking a bus. We're leaving at 3:00 p.m. from Portillo and we're arriving in Santiago at 6:00 p.m.

I love this festival because it's international. There are performances from about 20 countries! People watch shows in indoor and outdoor theaters. They also watch street performers and buy food and drinks from food stalls. Organizers work very hard to prepare for the festival because it's the most important cultural event in our country.

Do you want to come? You're in time – the festival lasts three weeks. And don't worry about tickets. Some street performances are free! *Martín, Chile*

This Sunday is January 5th and I'm going to the largest carnival celebration in southern Colombia, the Carnival of Blacks and Whites. My friends are coming to my home and we're walking to town together in black clothes.

The carnival lasts three days. On January 4th, there is a parade. Then January 5th is Blacks' Day, so we wear black clothes and black make-up. The next day is Whites' Day and we throw a lot of talcum powder into the air and over each other! There's also a parade. Performers play music very loudly and we all dance happily. We have a lot of fun!

What are you doing this Sunday? Are you doing anything special? *Valentina, Colombia*

2 Read for general ideas > Complete the chart with the main activities people do.

Santiago a Mil	The Carnival of Blacks and Whites

3 Read for details > Circle the correct options.

Santiago a Mil is an international (1) **festival / carnival**. It lasts three (2) **days / weeks**. Martín is going to the festival (3) **tomorrow / next weekend**. He's going by (4) **train / bus**.

People celebrate the Carnival of Blacks and Whites in the (5) **north / south** of Colombia. The celebrations last three (6) **days / weeks**.

WEB QUEST

Find out about a festival or a special day.

1 Choose a country and do an online search to find information about its festivals or special days.
2 Make notes in your notebook to answer these questions: Where? When? What?
3 Share the information with the class and say what you like about the festival.

#tip

Travel websites often have interesting information about carnivals and festivals.

Grammar
Present progressive for arrangements

USE

A Analyze these sentences from the text on page 70. Underline eight more examples of the present progressive.

My friends and I are going there tomorrow.

We're taking a bus.

We're leaving at 3:00 p.m. from Portillo and we're arriving in Santiago at about 6:00 p.m.

This Sunday is January 5th and I'm going to the largest carnival celebration in southern Colombia.

My friends are coming to my home and we're walking to town together in black clothes.

What are you doing this Sunday?

Are you doing anything special?

B Circle the correct option to complete the rule.

We use the **present progressive / simple present** to talk about specific plans with a fixed date or time in the future.

FORM

C Complete the chart.

Affirmative and negative

I	_____ / 'm not	leaving at 3:00 p.m.
He / She / It	's / isn't	
We / You / They	_____ / aren't	

Yes/No questions

Am	I	leaving at 6:00 p.m.?
Is	he / she / it	
_____	we / you / they	

Short answers

	I	am.
Yes,	he / she / it	_____.
	we / you / they	are.
	I	'm not.
No,	he / she / it	isn't.
	we / you / they	_____.

Wh- questions

What / When What time / Where	is	he / she / it	playing?
	_____	we / you / they	

D Complete the diagram.

To form the present progressive we need:

_____ + *-ing* form of a verb

1 Complete the conversation with the correct form of the verbs in parentheses.

Kay: Where (1) _____ (you / go) on vacation this year, Dan?
Dan: We (2) _____ (go) to Mexico – to Cancún.
Kay: Wow! That sounds great.
(3) _____ (you / fly) there?
Dan: Yes, we are.
Kay: Well, have fun! I (4) _____ (not go) on vacation this summer.
I (5) _____ (work) at a café for five weeks.
Dan: Oh, that's too bad!

2 Write questions.

1 Where / you / go / tonight?
_____

2 What / you / do / on Sunday afternoon?
_____

3 you / do / anything special / next week?
_____

3 Free practice > In turns, ask and answer about your arrangements. Use the time expressions from the box.

> tonight   on Saturday morning
> this weekend   on Friday evening
> on Sunday afternoon

🟠 *What are you doing tonight?*
🔵 *I'm going to the movies. What are you doing?*

71

Build your skills

Reading & Listening
A festival leaflet

1 Before you read > Look at the poster. Circle the activity from the box you can see in the pictures.

> Morris dancing   brass band   jousting   archery   Scout parade
> Medieval market   The battle of Saint George and the Dragon

Saint George's Day Festival
in Nottingham, England

Next Saturday 10:30–4:30

- 10:30 a.m.   Opening of the festival by the Mayor of Nottingham
- 11:30 a.m.   "The Battle of Saint George and the Dragon" at Nottingham Castle
- 12:30 p.m.   Morris dancers in the Market Square
- 1:30 p.m.   Archery and jousting at Nottingham Castle
- 2:30 p.m.   Brass band in the Market Square
- 3:30 p.m.   Scout parade through the city

FUN FOR ALL THE FAMILY!

There is also a Medieval market all day at the Market Square.
All events are FREE!

2 Read > Answer the questions.
1. Who is opening the festival?
2. What time are the Morris dancers starting?
3. Where are they doing the archery and jousting?
4. What time does the festival finish?
5. What is happening at 3:30 p.m.?

3 🔊 32 Listen to four teenagers from New York talking about going on a trip. Check (✓) four trips they mention.

1. a school trip to a museum
2. a day trip to Ellis Island
3. a trip to visit relatives in Albany
4. a Scout trip to the Catskill Mountains
5. a day trip to the beach on Coney Island
6. a day trip to an amusement park

4 🔊 32 Listen again. Underline the correct options.

1. Ann is going to visit the **Museum of Natural History** / **National Art Gallery**.
2. Ben is going to stay with his **grandparents** / **cousins**.
3. Charlotte is going to stay at a **youth hostel** / **campsite**.
4. David is going to travel by **car** / **bus**.

72

Listening & Speaking
Making arrangements

1 Before you listen > Look at the picture and make predictions. James and Hazel are making an arrangement. What is it about?

_____

_____

2 🔊 **33 Listen for general ideas >** Answer the questions.

1 What festival is Hazel going to?

_____

2 Can James come?

_____

3 🔊 **33 Listen for details >** Complete the conversation.

Hi there. What are you up to?	Oh, nothing special. I'm just going to (1) _____ .
Listen, are you free on (2) _____ ?	Yes, I think so. Why?
I'm going to the Harvest Festival, in Springfield. Do you want to (3) come _____ ?	That sounds fun. (4) _____ else is going?
My (5) _____ and my cousin Harry.	Great! What (6) _____ are you going?
We're leaving at (7) _____ .	OK. Can I meet you at your (8) _____ ?
Yes, sure. See you soon.	See you on Saturday!

4 Read > Role play in pairs.
1 Role play the conversation in Activity 3.
2 Role play a new conversation. Use other festivals or events.
3 Switch roles.

Keep it going!

Underline these phrases in the conversation.

Are you free on... ?   Yes, I think so.
I'm going to...   Do you want to come?
That sounds fun.   Who else is going?
What time are you going?   Can I...?

Remember to use them to make arrangements.

Writing
An invitation

1 Read the invitation. Where is Brad from? What is the invitation for?

It's Independence Day on July 4th and we're having a party – we hope you can come!

Hello all,

The party is at our house in Washington, on Saturday. It starts at 5 o'clock in the afternoon. We're going to have a barbecue (Dad is great at making barbecues!). After that, we're going to watch the fireworks. The weather should be good. It's always warm and sunny in July.

All my cousins from Florida are coming, too. It's going to be a lot of fun! Let me know if you can come. And don't forget to wear red, white, and blue!

See you soon!

Brad

PS: We're decorating the garden in the morning – do you want to come and help?

---

2 Read the "Write it right!" section.

Write it right!
Prepositions of time and place

⤳ Pay attention to these prepositions.

in	towns / cities / states months / seasons parts of the day	in Washington in July / in the summer in the afternoon
on	days dates	on Saturday on July 4th
at	places times	at our house at 5 o'clock

3 Look at the invitation again. Circle the prepositions *in*, *on*, and *at*.

4 Complete the sentences with *in*, *on*, or *at*.

1 My birthday is _____ March 3rd.
2 We're having dinner _____ 8 o'clock.
3 My relatives are coming _____ the morning.
4 What are you doing _____ Friday?
5 He's on vacation _____ Paris.
6 We're going to have a party _____ the youth club.

Writing task

Plan > Imagine it's your birthday next week and you want to have a party. Make notes in your notebook to answer these questions: Where? When? What time? What activities? What food?

Write > Write your invitation. Remember to use:
- vocabulary on celebrations.
- *going to* to express intentions or the present progressive for arrangements.
- the correct prepositions of time and place.

Check > Check your writing.

The Beat MAGAZINE

The Edinburgh Fringe

It's August and our special columnist, Anthony Murphy, traveled to Scotland for the amazing Edinburgh Fringe, the most exciting festival in the world!

This is Anthony Murphy reporting from Edinburgh. The best festival in the UK is starting in a few days and it's going to be great!

Last week, I bought tickets for the big acts and this is my plan. On Saturday, I'm going to walk around the city. I'm going to see a lot of street performers, circus acts, dancers, and singers. On Saturday night, I'm going to see a famous comedian at the Pleasance Theater. I'm very excited! You can see comedy, art, dance, theater, and music for free.

Why is the Edinburgh Fringe special?

- It's the biggest festival of theater, comedy, music and dance in the world.
- Performers from all over the world take part in it. There aren't any rules to participate in the festival. Anyone can put on a show.
- It takes place all over the city of Edinburgh – at theaters, on the streets, at cafés, and at people's homes! A lot of performances are free.
- It's on for three weeks every August.

Are you planning to come? Here are my tips:

- You're going to do a lot of walking, so wear sneakers. The weather can be windy, rainy, cold, cloudy, warm, and sunny, all in one day! So bring an umbrella, a bottle of water and wear sunglasses.
- Go to the small cafés and restaurants in the city. Some of the best comedy is there and it's free!
- Watch the fireworks from Princess Street Gardens. They're amazing and you don't need to buy tickets.

---

1 🔊 **34** Listen and read the article. What is the Edinburgh Fringe?

_____

2 Read again and circle *T* (True) or *F* (False). Correct the false sentences in your notebook.

1 Anthony Murphy traveled to England.   T   F
2 He bought tickets yesterday.   T   F
3 He doesn't want to walk around the city.   T   F
4 He's going to watch street performances.   T   F
5 He's going to see a comedy show in a restaurant.   T   F
6 The weather in Edinburgh is usually warm and sunny in August.   T   F

3 👤 Choose one of these activities.

1 In your notebook, write a list of things you like about the Edinburgh Fringe. Compare lists with a classmate.
2 Draw a mind map about the Edinburgh Fringe in your notebook. Compare mind maps with a classmate.

UNIT 6 Take care

Vocabulary
Physical and mental health

1. 🔊 35 Add *don't* where necessary to complete the tips about physical and mental health. Then listen, check, and repeat.

   1 _____ exercise regularly
   2 _____ discuss your worries
   3 _____ get into arguments
   4 _____ take time for yourself
   5 _____ get stressed about tests
   6 _____ ask for help
   7 _____ worry about your appearance
   8 _____ try new sports
   9 _____ bully other people
   10 _____ eat a healthy diet

2. Read the web page. Complete the text with verbs from Activity 1.

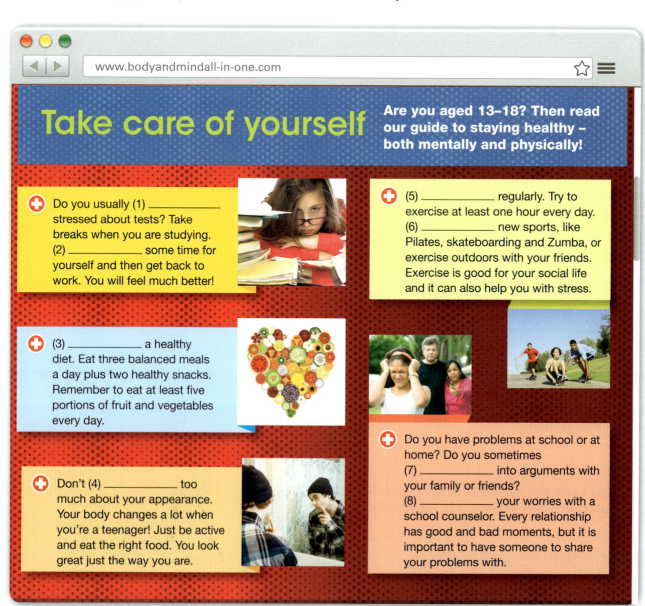

www.bodyandmindall-in-one.com

Take care of yourself
Are you aged 13–18? Then read our guide to staying healthy – both mentally and physically!

✚ Do you usually (1) _____ stressed about tests? Take breaks when you are studying. (2) _____ some time for yourself and then get back to work. You will feel much better!

✚ (3) _____ a healthy diet. Eat three balanced meals a day plus two healthy snacks. Remember to eat at least five portions of fruit and vegetables every day.

✚ Don't (4) _____ too much about your appearance. Your body changes a lot when you're a teenager! Just be active and eat the right food. You look great just the way you are.

✚ (5) _____ regularly. Try to exercise at least one hour every day. (6) _____ new sports, like Pilates, skateboarding and Zumba, or exercise outdoors with your friends. Exercise is good for your social life and it can also help you with stress.

✚ Do you have problems at school or at home? Do you sometimes (7) _____ into arguments with your family or friends? (8) _____ your worries with a school counselor. Every relationship has good and bad moments, but it is important to have someone to share your problems with.

76

3 Complete the sentences about the pictures with the tips from Activity 1. Pay attention to verb forms.

These students _____ all the time.

Jess _____.

Nick _____.

Sam _____ with her parents.

Jake _____. He meditates every day.

Mel and Bea _____. They go jogging twice a week.

4 Organize the words in the box according to the tip from Activity 1 they are related to.

> avoid fat and sugar   do yoga
> drink lots of water   go jogging
> share your problems with a good friend
> study for tests in advance
> talk to your parents
> talk to your teacher about your questions

Exercise regularly	
Eat a healthy diet	
Ask for help	
Don't get stressed about tests	

5 Give your opinion > Which tip from Activity 1 do you like best? Why? Share your ideas with a classmate.

_____
_____

6 Answer the questions.

1 Do you take time for yourself?
_____

2 Do you usually get stressed about tests?
_____

3 Do you eat a healthy diet?
_____

4 Do you exercise every day?
_____

5 Do you sometimes get into arguments with your family or friends?
_____

6 Do you worry about your appearance?
_____

7 In turns, ask and answer the questions from Activity 6. Ask other questions to find out more.

- *Do you take time for yourself?*
- *Yes, I do.*
- *What do you do?*
- *I listen to my favorite music and dance!*

LEARNING TO LEARN

It's easier to remember new vocabulary when you see it every day. Make a small poster with tips for staying healthy and put it in your bedroom.

Reading
An information leaflet

1 Before you read > Look at the leaflet quickly. What is it about? What is the girl in the picture worried about?

CYBERBULLYING AND HOW TO DEAL WITH IT

Is someone sending you nasty messages or posting rude comments about you on the Internet? Should you reply or should you ignore them? Here's some useful advice.

1. Don't reply. Bullies want to get a reaction from you, so you shouldn't show them that you're angry or upset. When someone bullies you in a chat room, for example, you shouldn't get into an argument with him or her. You should report the messages to the chat room moderator.

2. Stop the communication. If you can't live without your cell phone or social network for a few days, use filters to block unkind messages. You should also block phone numbers on your cell phone.

3. Ask for help immediately. It is very difficult to deal with bullying without help from an adult. You should discuss your worries with your parents, a teacher, or the school counselor.

4. Save the evidence. Take screenshots and save messages from the cyberbully and then show them to an adult. He or she will help you to deal with that and take any further measures.

5. Take action to help other people. Is a friend receiving nasty messages? Give him or her some of these tips. Is there a bully in your group? You shouldn't be afraid to report him or her.

HOW TO AVOID CYBERBULLYING?

6. Protect your personal information. You shouldn't share your cell phone number or email address with people you don't know. Also, you should be careful about accepting new friends or contacts on social networking sites or apps.

7. Learn how to report bullying behavior to administrators and/or moderators on social networks, chat rooms, and apps. Immediate action from administrators usually stops bullies before they cause more damage.

8. Never share your passwords with friends. The only people who should know your passwords and have access to your accounts are your parents.

9. Do you want to post your picture or video online? You should think carefully before doing that. Once content goes online, it is very difficult to predict how people share it or the comments they make about it.

Bullying ruins people's lives. Victims of bullying often feel sad or depressed. They have low confidence because they think that they are the problem.

Do people bully you? Remember: the problem is NOT you – it's them. So don't be afraid to talk about it and ask for help!

If you need help, contact the Stop Cyberbullying Helpline: 800 789 8421

2 Read for general ideas > Answer the questions.

1 What is cyberbullying?
   _____
   _____

2 What does "bully" mean?
   _____
   _____

3 Why is it important to learn how to report bullying behavior?
   _____
   _____

4 In cases of bullying, who is the problem: the bully or the victim of bullying?
   _____
   _____

5 Why is it important to stop bullies?
   _____
   _____

3 Read for details > Circle T (True) or F (False). Correct the false sentences.

1 Bullies want to get replies from their victims. T F
   _____
   _____

2 If you receive nasty messages, you have to reply immediately. T F
   _____
   _____

3 The leaflet advises to stop communication with bullies. T F
   _____
   _____

4 It's good to delete messages from bullies. T F
   _____
   _____

5 It's not a good idea to give your cell phone number to strangers. T F
   _____
   _____

6 It's not a good idea to give access to your accounts to your parents. T F
   _____
   _____

7 It's important to be careful about posting your pictures and videos online. T F
   _____
   _____

8 Victims of bullying usually know that they are not the problem. T F
   _____
   _____

4 Read for inference > Read these questions from teens on the helpline. Match them to the advice on the leaflet.

"Hello. My name's Sarah and a person I know is sending nasty messages to me on WhatsApp. I want to delete them."

"Hi! My best friend wants to have access to my account on Instagram, but I'm not sure this is a good idea. Passwords are private, right?"

"Hi, it's Josh here. A boy from my school is posting offensive comments about a girl in our class. I feel I should help the girl and tell an adult about it, but I'm not sure."

"Hey, This is Cathy. A bully from the gym keeps calling me on my cell phone. I don't want to talk to him, but I don't know what to do. I can't turn off my phone, you know…"

Find out more information on a website.

1 Visit www.stopbullying.gov and stopbullyingnow.com, and choose one.
2 Read some information and make notes in your notebook.
3 Share your notes with the class.

#tip

A website contains a lot of information, so choose a topic you're interested in and read about it.

Grammar
Should: affirmative, negative, and questions

USE

A Analyze these sentences from the text on page 78. Underline five more examples of *should*.

<u>Should</u> you <u>reply</u>?

You shouldn't show them that you're angry.

You shouldn't get into an argument.

You should report the messages to the chat room moderator.

You should also block phone numbers on your cell phone.

You should discuss your worries with your parents, a teacher, or a school counselor.

B Check (✓) the correct option to complete the rule.

We use *should* to give:
- orders. ☐
- advice. ☐

FORM

C Complete the charts.

Affirmative			
I / You / He / She / It / We / They	should	save	messages.

Negative			
I / You / He / She / It / We / They	_____	save	messages.

Yes/No questions			
_____	I / you / he / she / it / we / they	save	messages?

Short answers			
Yes,	I / you / he / she / it / we / they	_____.	
No,		shouldn't.	

D Check (✓) the correct option.

You should go. ☐
You should to go. ☐

---

1 Complete the sentences with *should* or *shouldn't*.

1 You _____ spend so much time on the computer.
2 Rosie _____ shout at her little sister.
3 I _____ do Zumba. It sounds fun.
4 We _____ be friendly to the new girl in school.
5 You _____ bully your classmates.

2 Write questions using *should* to ask for advice.

1 we / order / a pizza?
   _____

2 they / tell someone / about the problem?
   _____

3 Vicky / go to the movies / with Matt?
   _____

4 you / paint / your bedroom black?
   _____

3 👤 Free practice > Use *should* or *shouldn't* to write a piece of advice for each problem in your notebook. Share your ideas with the class.

1 I always get stressed about tests.
2 I don't have many friends. I want to make new friends.
3 I can't get up in the mornings and I'm often late to school.
4 I always get into arguments with my brother.
5 Someone is sending me nasty messages on my cell phone.

COMPARING LANGUAGES

Translate into your language:
You should ask for help.
How do you say *should* in your language?

80

Vocabulary
Health problems and first aid

1 🔊 36 Read the first aid kit advice. Listen and repeat the words in blue.

TRAVEL WISELY: TAKE A FIRST AID KIT WITH YOU!

Dr. Maggie gives you advice about what to take.

- Remember to take some **adhesive bandages** with you. Travelers often get **blisters** on their feet because they walk too much during their vacation.
- **Sunburn** never looks good! You should always put some **sunscreen** on your skin before you go out in the sun.
- Take some **aspirins**. In the summer, heat can give you a **headache**. In the winter, aspirins can help you if you catch a **cold**.
- Do you always get **mosquito bites** in tropical countries? Remember to take some **insect repellent** to spray over you when you go out at night.
- Take some **antacid** with you. Do you sometimes get a **stomachache** when you're traveling? You should have antacid. It can help you to feel better.

Put all these things in your suitcase, but also carry some of them in your backpack. And remember: wear your backpack on both shoulders so you don't get a **backache**!

Do you have a health problem and don't know what to do about it? Email Dr. Maggie or call our teen helpline on 800 475 6354.

2 Classify the words in blue.

Health problems	First aid kit items

3 👤 Answer the questions.

1 What first aid kit items do you usually take when you go on a trip?

_____

2 What health problems from the article do you sometimes have? What do you do to feel better?

_____
_____

COMPARING CULTURES

In your country, do you need a medical prescription to buy any of the first aid items in the text?

Listening
Helpline

4 🔊 37 Listen to two phone calls to Dr. Maggie's helpline. Complete the sentences with health problems from the box.

> a cold   a headache
> a stomachache   a backache

1 David has _____.
2 Molly has _____.

5 🔊 37 Listen again. Answer the questions.

1 How does David go to school?
_____

2 According to Dr. Maggie, how should he carry his bag?
_____

3 Why is Molly getting headaches?
_____

4 What is Dr. Maggie's advice?
_____
_____

Reading
A magazine article

1 Before you read > What do you know about Machu Picchu? What is it? Where is it?

_____

VISIT MACHU PICCHU IN PERU
SOUTH AMERICA'S MOST POPULAR ATTRACTION

Machu Picchu is 2,430 m above sea level. The Incas created this city about 550 years ago. Today, impressive ruins, very high mountains, and subtropical forests make this place a perfect destination.

Are you planning a trip to this popular attraction? Read the questions from our readers and the answers from our travel experts!

Why should I bring Peruvian money? Can't I use my credit card?

You should bring Peruvian money to buy souvenirs from local artisans or bottled water and snacks from small stores. You can use credit cards in big stores, hotels, and restaurants. The local money is the *sol*. You should always have about 100 or 200 *soles* with you.

When is the best time to visit Machu Picchu? Why should I go in the high season? Why should I go in the low season?

Machu Picchu has a dry season (May–October) and a wet season (November–April). Most tourists don't visit Machu Picchu during the wet season because it rains most of the days. You can choose the season you prefer. You should come in the high season to enjoy lots of sunny days. You should come in the low season to avoid the crowds.

What kind of clothes should I pack?

In Machu Picchu, it can be very hot during the day and very cold at night, so bring a pair of shorts to be comfortable during the day and a pair of pants and a jacket to keep warm when the sun sets. Hiking boots or sneakers are essential. You need them to explore the ruins and climb mountains.

What shouldn't I forget?

Bring sunscreen to protect your skin from the sun. Bring a camera to take pictures and binoculars to observe wildlife and distant places. There are sand flies, so a good repellent is very important. And don't forget to bring a comfortable backpack to carry your things with you during the day.

2 Read for general ideas > Answer the questions.

1 Where are the ruins?
_____

2 How old are they?
_____

3 What is the local money in Peru?
_____

4 When do most tourists visit the ruins?
_____

5 What are some useful items to pack?
_____
_____

3 Read for details > Correct the sentences.

1 Local artisans accept credit cards.
_____

2 The dry season starts in November.
_____

3 The wet season ends in October.
_____

4 It's usually cold during the day.
_____

4 Give your opinion > Would you like to travel to Machu Picchu? Why (not)? Discuss with your classmates.

Grammar
The infinitive of purpose

USE

A Analyze these sentences from the text on page 82. Underline five more infinitives of purpose.

You should bring Peruvian money to buy souvenirs from local artisans.

You should come in the high season to enjoy lots of sunny days.

Bring a pair of shorts and T-shirts to be comfortable during the day.

You need them to explore the ruins.

Bring sunscreen to protect your skin from the sun.

Bring a camera to take pictures.

B Analyze these questions and answers. Underline two infinitives of purpose.

Why should I bring Peruvian money?
To buy bottled water from small stores.

Why should I come in the low season?
To avoid the crowds.

C Look at Activities A and B again. Find and write an example for each rule.

We can use the infinitive of purpose in a complete sentence to give the purpose of an action.

_____

_____

We can use the infinitive of purpose in an incomplete sentence to answer the question "Why?".

_____?

_____.

FORM

D We use *to* + infinitive to form the infinitive of purpose. Check (✓) the correct sentences.

I need a backpack **carry** my things. ☐
I need a backpack **to carry** my things. ☐
Why did you go to the stores?
To buy a souvenir. ☐
Why did you go to the stores?
For buy a souvenir. ☐

---

1 Complete the sentences with the correct infinitive of purpose. Use the verbs from the box.

> take   climb   find   carry   protect   tell

1. You should put some sunscreen on _____ your skin.
2. Travel in the low season _____ cheaper prices.
3. I want to buy a new camera _____ better pictures.
4. You should create a blog _____ your friends about your adventures.
5. I want to buy a comfortable backpack _____ all my things.
6. Wear comfortable shoes _____ that mountain.

2 Match the answers to the questions.

1. Why did she call the hospital? ☐
2. Why did he go to the supermarket? ☐
3. Why do they want to go to Europe? ☐

a To visit Italy.
b To make an appointment with the doctor.
c To buy some snacks.

3 Free practice > Complete the notes. Then write sentences.

1. Something I want to have: _____
   Purpose: _____
2. Something I want to do: _____
   Purpose: _____
3. A place I want to visit: _____
   Purpose: _____

83

Build your skills

Reading & Listening
An online ad

1 Before you read > Look at the ad. What is the name of the new app?

_____

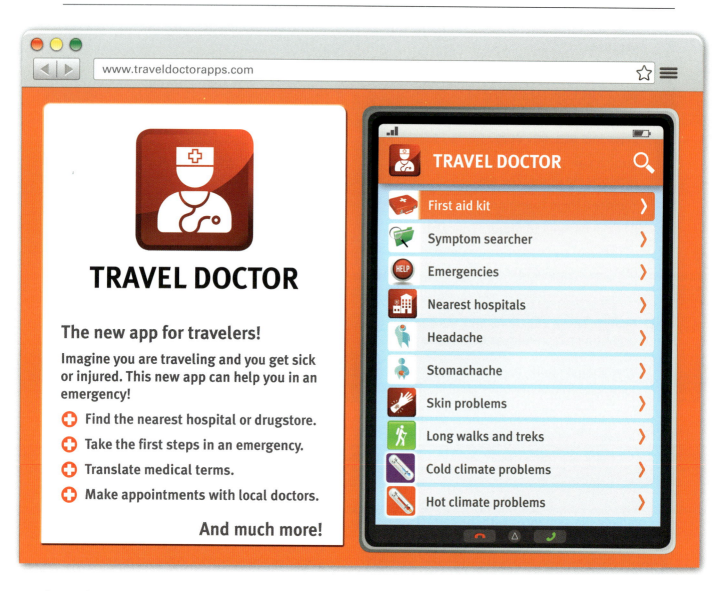

2 Read > Answer the questions.

1 Who is this app for?
_____

2 What can it help you to find?
_____

3 What does it give advice about?
_____

3 🔊 38 Listen to two friends talking about the "Travel Doctor" app. Answer the questions.

1 Who has the new app: the girl or the boy?
_____

2 What is the boy doing in August?
_____

4 🔊 38 Listen again. Circle the correct answers.

1 The boy wants to use the app in his...
   a summer vacation.   b winter vacation.

2 The boy says the app has a video about...
   a mosquito bites.   b snake bites.

3 The boy says the app can help you to find the nearest...
   a hospital.   b drugstore.

Listening & Speaking
Talking about health

1 Before you listen > Look at the picture. Where are they? What do you think the girl is buying?

_____

_____

2 🔊 39 **Listen for general ideas** > Answer the questions.

1 What health problem does the girl have?

_____

2 What does she buy?

_____

3 🔊 39 **Listen for details** > Complete the conversation.

Hi there. What's the (1) _____?	I have some mosquito bites on my (2) _____.
Oh! When did that happen?	They bit me (3) _____ when I was at the (4) _____.
Oh, no! How do you (5) _____?	I feel (6) _____, but they're really painful.
Right. I think you should use this (7) _____ on the bites and make a doctor's appointment if they get (8) _____.	Yes, I'll do that. How much is this?
It's (9) _____.	OK. Here you go.
I hope you feel better soon!	Thanks!

4 Speak > Role play in pairs.

1 Role play the conversation in Activity 3.
2 Role play a new conversation. Use other health problems.
3 Switch roles.

Keep it going!

Underline these statements / questions in the conversation.

What's the matter?   **When did that happen?**
How do you feel?   **I feel OK.**
I hope you feel better soon.

Remember to use them to talk about health problems.

Writing
Emails

1 Read Johnny's email and Tilda's reply. What is Johnny's problem? Do you agree with Tilda's advice? Discuss with your classmates.

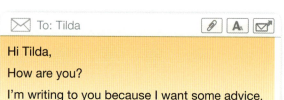

To: Tilda

Hi Tilda,

How are you?

I'm writing to you because I want some advice. I want to go to a summer camp for teenagers in August, but my parents don't let me go. They think I should go on vacation with them, but I know it's going to be really boring!

What should I do?

Johnny

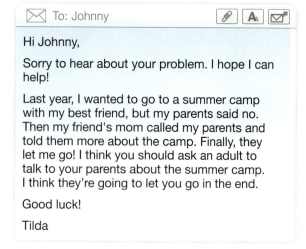

To: Johnny

Hi Johnny,

Sorry to hear about your problem. I hope I can help!

Last year, I wanted to go to a summer camp with my best friend, but my parents said no. Then my friend's mom called my parents and told them more about the camp. Finally, they let me go! I think you should ask an adult to talk to your parents about the summer camp. I think they're going to let you go in the end.

Good luck!

Tilda

3 Read Tilda's reply again. Answer the questions.

1 Does Tilda give an example of a similar situation?
_____

2 Where did Tilda want to go last year?
_____

3 Who called Tilda's parents? Why?
_____
_____

4 What happened in the end?
_____

2 Read the "Write it right!" section.

Write it right!
Asking for and giving advice

Asking for advice	Giving advice
I'm writing to you because I want some advice.	Sorry to hear about your problem.
What should I do?	I hope I can help!
	I think you should…
	Good luck!

Writing task

Step 1

Plan > Think of an imaginary problem.

Write > Write an email (in your notebook or using an email software) asking for advice. Remember to use:

- vocabulary on physical and mental health from this unit.
- phrases from the "Write it right!" section.

Check > Check your writing.

Step 2

Write > Exchange emails with a classmate. Write a reply to his/her email. Remember to:

- give an example of a similar situation and say what happened.
- use phrases from the "Write it right!" section.
- use *should* to give advice.

Check > Check your writing.

The Beat MAGAZINE

The outback survival guide

If you're planning a trip to the Australian Outback, you should read this guide to stay safe!

The Outback is a large desert area of Australia. Very few people live there and temperatures can be very high – about 50°C in summer! Read these tips and travel wisely.

Do's

- Take water to survive. There aren't many places where you can find water in the Outback. The heat makes you thirsty and you should drink several liters of water a day. You can survive for many days without food, but not without water!
- Wear a hat and use sunscreen to avoid sunburn. The sun is one of the biggest dangers in Australia. You should only hike in the morning and in the evening because it's very hot between 1:00 p.m. and 5:00 p.m.
- Plan your route carefully to make sure you get to your destination. You should take a map and a GPS. You should also tell a friend or relative about your plans – where you are going and when you are planning to get there.

Dont's

- Don't worry too much about snakes. There are many different kinds of poisonous snakes in Australia, but they don't usually attack people. Leave them alone and they aren't going to hurt you.
- Don't rely on your cell phone. Some of the areas in the Outback are very remote and there is no signal.
- Don't swim in deep, muddy water. There are dangerous crocodiles in Australia and they often attack people. Pay attention to crocodile warning signs!
- Don't leave your car if it breaks down. Your car can help a plane to find you. It's much easier to spot a car than a person from the air.

---

1 🔊 40 Listen and read about the Outback. Where is this place?

_____

2 Read again and answer.

1 What is the Outback?

_____

2 Why should you put sunscreen on?

_____

3 Why is it important to plan your route?

_____
_____

4 Why shouldn't you worry too much about snakes?

_____

5 Why shouldn't you swim in muddy waters?

_____
_____

3 👤 Choose one of these activities.

1 In your notebook, write a paragraph explaining why you want or don't want to visit the Outback.

2 Write five false sentences about the text on a slip of paper. Exchange slips with a classmate and correct the sentences.

PROGRESS CHECK — UNIT 5

Vocabulary
Celebrations

1 Complete the verbs for celebrations.

1 Do you always d_____ your house for Christmas?
2 People w_____ black and white clothes for the Carnival of Blacks and Whites.
3 I like e_____ special food on my birthday. We usually have a barbecue.
4 My little brother thinks Santa Claus g_____ children presents on Christmas.
5 It's your birthday next week. Are you going to h_____ a party?
6 Thanksgiving is a time to be with the family, so we always v_____ relatives.
7 Do you w_____ fireworks on New Year's Eve?
8 On Halloween, I go out with friends and we h_____ a lot of fun.

/ 8 points

Adverbs of manner

2 Complete the sentences with adverbs.

1 He was traveling at 150 km per hour. He was driving _____!
2 My sister plays the violin really _____. She is going to be an excellent musician.
3 You shouldn't eat so much chocolate. You should eat _____!
4 They play very _____. I think they are not going to win.
5 Do you want to pass your tests? Then you need to work _____!
6 He can't hear us because he's playing the music very _____.

/ 6 points

Grammar

Going to

3 Complete the sentences with the correct form of *going to* and the verbs in parentheses.

1 Next year, I _____ (not go) to the gym once a week. I _____ (exercise) more regularly!
2 What _____ (you / do) during your vacation?
3 She _____ (not have) a birthday party. She _____ (go) on a trip with her family.
4 Where _____ (they / celebrate) Mother's Day?
5 They _____ (not buy) tickets for the concert.

/ 7 points

Object pronouns

4 Complete the sentences and questions with the correct object pronouns.

1 This is for Emily. Can you give it to _____?
2 Do you know his address? I want to send _____ a card.
3 We want to go to the festival. Can you take _____ to the train station?
4 Look at those dancers! Take a picture of _____!

/ 4 points

Present progressive for arrangements

5 Complete the conversation with the present progressive form of the verbs in parentheses.

Jay: What (1) _____ (you / do) tonight?
Brad: Nothing special. And you?
Jay: I (2) _____ (go) to a music festival. Do you want to come?
Brad: Yes! Who else (3) _____ (go)?
Jay: Joe. We (4) _____ (leave) at 8 p.m.
Brad: (5) _____ (you / leave) from your house?
Jay: Yes. See you there at 8 p.m.!
Brad: OK!

/ 5 points

Check your performance!

Try again! 0–9   Keep up! 10–16   Well done! 17–23   Great job! 24–30

Total Score: _____ / 30 points

UNIT 6 PROGRESS CHECK

Vocabulary
Physical and mental health

1 Complete the sentences with the verbs from the box.

> take   try   bully   ask   get (x2)

1 Don't _____ stressed about tests. _____ some time for yourself.
2 You should _____ new sports. Exercise is good for the body and mind.
3 When people _____ you and send you nasty messages, it is not a good idea to _____ into arguments with them. You should _____ for help.

/ 6 points

Health problems

2 Complete the sentences with words for health problems.

1. He always gets a _____ because he carries his school bag on one shoulder.
2. You can get _____ on your feet when you wear new shoes.
3. Don't spend too many hours on your computer. It can give you a _____.
4. I always get a _____ when I eat a lot of unhealthy food.

☐ / 4 points

First aid kit

3 Look at the picture and write words for first aid items.

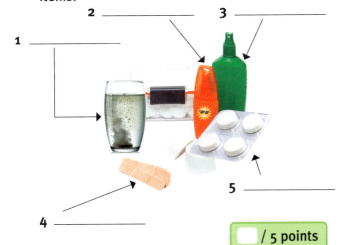

1 _____
2 _____
3 _____
4 _____
5 _____

☐ / 5 points

Grammar

Should

4 Complete the statements and questions with the correct form of *should* and the verbs in parentheses.

1. You _____ (be) nice to your brothers and sisters.
2. He _____ (not get) angry with his parents. They are trying to help.
3. _____ (I / pack) summer or winter clothes?
4. She _____ (not post) pictures of people without permission.
5. Where _____ (we / buy) the tickets?

☐ / 5 points

5 Write a piece of advice for each problem.

1. **Sally:** I feel tired. I want to have more energy.
   You: _____
2. **Ben:** I'm not doing very well in school.
   You: _____
3. **Thomas:** Someone is posting rude comments about me.
   You: _____

☐ / 3 points

The infinitive of purpose

6 Complete the sentences with infinitives of purpose.

1. He went to the travel agency _____ a plane ticket.
2. You can use this app _____ drugstores and hospitals.
3. You should wear hiking boots _____ mountains.
4. I need a sheet of paper _____ a list.

☐ / 4 points

7 Answer the questions. Use infinitives of purpose.

1. Why are you reading that article?
   _____
2. Why did she go to the shopping mall?
   _____
3. Why does he want to buy a bicycle?
   _____

☐ / 3 points

Check your performance!

Try again! 0–9 Keep up! 10–16 Well done! 17–23 Great job! 24–30

Total Score: ☐ / 30 points

NOTES

UNIT 1 — What do you like?

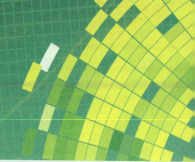

Vocabulary
Free-time activities

1 Match the columns.

1	go	a	the Internet
2	watch	b	text messages
3	surf	c	shopping
4	hang out	d	volleyball
5	listen	e	a DVD
6	send	f	for a run
7	chat	g	water sports
8	go	h	with friends
9	do	i	to music
10	play	j	online

(1–c matched)

2 Order the letters to find adjectives.

1. RINFLEDY — _friendly_
2. AZYL — _____
3. BOCLASEI — _____
4. NEFLIRDUNY — _____
5. HYS — _____
6. CAVITE — _____

3 Write an adjective from Activity 2 for each speech bubble.

I hang out with my friends on Saturdays.
1. _friendly_

I love meeting new friends!
2. _____

I don't go to parties. I don't speak to anyone.
3. _____

Friends? I don't have any.
4. _____

We play volleyball or go for a run on Sundays.
5. _____

I never clean my room or help at home.
6. _____

Grammar
Simple present and present progressive

4 Write affirmative or negative sentences, or questions.

1. we / go for a run / on Saturdays (✗)
   We don't go for a run on Saturdays.
2. you / listen to reggae music / now (?)
   _____
3. Sandra / usually / meet friends / on Sundays (✓)
   _____
4. I / read a great novel / at the moment (✓)
   _____

5 Complete with the correct form of the verbs in parentheses.

Hi, there! I'm Annette. I (1) _live_ (live) in Bourbon, Indiana with my family but at the moment, I (2) _____ (live) in New York. I (3) _____ (study) languages at a very big language school in Manhattan.

In my free time, I always (4) _____ (go) for a run at Central Park or (5) _____ (play) volleyball at the sports center opposite my apartment. But today, I am tired. I am at home. I (6) _____ (chat) online with my friends in Indiana and I (7) _____ (listen) to music. I like reggae.

6 Write questions about Annette.

1. Where / live?
   Where does Annette live?
2. What / do / New York / at the moment?
   _____
3. What / do / free time?
   _____
4. Where / play / volleyball?
   _____

94

UNIT 1

Vocabulary
Skills and abilities

7 Complete the phrases.

1. _jump_ high
2. _____ a car
3. _____ a BMX bike
4. _____ a picture
5. _____ French
6. _____ a song
7. _____ a vegetable pie
8. _____ a wall
9. _____ a cartoon character
10. _____ English with friends

8 Complete the sentences with the correct form of the verbs from the box.

| act   climb (x2)   cook   draw   drive |
| jump   play   ~~ride~~   sing   speak |

1. My friend Richard usually __rides__ his BMX bike in the mountains. It's risky!
2. Jess _____ the drums in the school band. They sound marvelous.
3. Alec _____ old melodies in English at the moment. I love listening to him.
4. The Bronx brothers can _____ walls very easily. They want to _____ Aconcagua some day.
5. Dolphins can _____ very high in the air. I enjoy watching them.
6. Can you _____ English well?
7. Mom's in the kitchen now. She _____ my favorite meal.
8. My son _____ comics. He's really creative.
9. I can't _____ my father's car. I am only 13 years old.
10. Some students _____ out a conversation in front of their teacher. They are very nervous.

Grammar
love, hate, (don't) like, don't mind, enjoy + -ing

9 Order the words from the box from negative (-) to positive (+).

| don't like   don't mind   like   love   ~~hate~~ |

hate _____ _____ _____ _____

10 Circle the correct options.

Alan: Let's go to the park. There's a parkour competition.
Charlie: I (1) **don't mind** / **(don't like)** parkour. It's really dangerous.
Alan: I (2) **love** / **hate** watching parkour but I (3) **like** / **don't like** practicing it.
Charlie: I (4) **like** / **hate** swimming. It's relaxing.
Alan: Yes, I (5) **love** / **hate** it, too.
Alice: What do you want to do on Saturday evening?
Jordan: I (6) **don't mind** / **like** horror movies. Let's watch a DVD.
Alice: I don't (7) **mind** / **like** horror movies. They are scary! Let's watch a musical.
Jordan: I (8) **love** / **hate** musicals. I think they are really boring.
Alice: Do you want to invite your friends to play some music?
Jordan: Yes! I (9) **love** / **don't mind** singing and playing the guitar.

11 Complete the chart for you. Then write sentences in your notebook.

	Ralph	Rachel and Helen	My father	You
☺☺☺	play drums	sing in a choir	run	
☺☺		paint and draw	play soccer	
☺	sing		swim	
☹		do sports		
☹☹☹	dance	drive race cars	do urban sports	

Ralph loves playing the drums. He doesn't mind singing, but he hates dancing.

Reading
A TV interview

12 Read the interview. Then circle the correct option.

The Teens for Teen TV show host, Mark Allerton, is interviewing Josh.

Mark: Any plans for this summer vacation?
Josh: Well, I'm going to Orangers Activity Camp.
Mark: Why are you going there?
Josh: I love making new friends and having fun. I don't like sleeping all day long when I'm on vacation. It's boring!
Mark: What can you do at Orangers?
Josh: We can go swimming and sailing. I'm not very good at swimming, but I enjoy playing in the water.
Mark: Do you get up early?
Josh: Of course I do. In the mornings, we go trekking and we take pictures. I don't mind walking a lot. I love taking pictures. I am good at taking pictures of birds and butterflies.
Mark: What can you do in the evenings?
Josh: We work on creative writing. I love writing poems. We sit around a fire and we read. It's great!
Mark: Have a great time, Josh!

Mark and Josh are talking about
weekend activities / urban sports.

13 Read again and complete.

Josh…

loves _____

doesn't like _____

doesn't mind _____

is good at _____

isn't very good at _____

14 Read again and answer.

1 Where are Mark and Josh?
_____

2 What is Orangers?
_____

3 When is Josh going there?
_____

4 Does Josh like water sports?
_____

5 What animals can Josh photograph?
_____

6 When do they write poems?
_____

Speaking
Asking for personal information

15 Choose the correct option to complete the conversation.

Fred: Hello. I'd like (1) ___to register___ for one of your adventure weekends.
Travel agent: OK, great! I just need a few details from you. (2) _____?
Fred: Fred Collins.
Travel agent: And (3) _____, Fred?
Fred: 457 Oak St.
Travel agent: Right. What's your (4) _____ number?
Fred: 555-8902.
Travel agent: OK. (5) _____ email address?
Fred: Yes. It's fred_16@yupi.com.
Travel agent: Can you (6) _____ me?
Fred: Yes. It's f-r-e-d underscore sixteen at yupi dot com.
Travel agent: Great, thanks. Oh! What's (7) _____?
Fred: May 20th, 2002.
Travel agent: Thank you. Here you have more information about the camp.

1 a to register
   b to write
   c to speak
2 a What your name
   b What's your name
   c What do you do
3 a what's your house
   b what's your address
   c where's your address
4 a ID
   b student card
   c cell phone
5 a Is there a
   b Do you have an
   c Do you have a
6 a spell that for
   b write that to
   c say it to
7 a the date birth
   b your birthday
   c your date of birth

Writing
A personal profile

16 Read Chandler Riggs's profile and complete his fact file.

CHANDLER RIGGS

Hi! My name's Chandler Riggs and I'm 17 years old*. I'm from Atlanta, in the USA. I live with my mom and dad. I don't have any brothers or sisters. My best friends are Olivia and Peter.

I like music, so I listen to music all the time. I can play the drums. I love acting. I'm an actor in a TV series. I enjoy scary roles. I'm studying a new story at the moment.

I also love practicing sports because I am active. I like rollerblading and mountain biking. I love going shopping, but I don't buy expensive clothes.

*in 2016

FACT FILE

Name	
Date of birth	June 27th, 1999
Place of birth	
Occupation	
Popular for	*The Walking Dead*
Family	father – William Riggs mother – Gina Carlton
Likes	

17 Copy the fact file from Activity 16 into your notebook and complete it with information about a friend. Then write his/her personal profile.

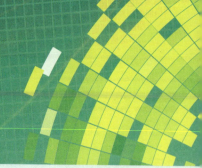

UNIT 2 Music and TV

Vocabulary
Music

1 Circle the odd one out.

1. piano – keyboards – (choir) – harmonica
2. composer – classical – orchestra – singer
3. violin – rock – pop – R&B
4. singer – drums – conductor – backing vocals
5. dance – bass – latin – rap
6. rap – rock – guitar – classical

2 Complete the chart with words from Activity 1.

Types of music	classical
Instruments	
Musicians	

3 Order the letters to make words to complete the text.

My favorite (1) **dabn** ___band___ is Walk the Moon. There are four members in it. All of them are (2) **grisens** _____. Nicholas Petricca plays the (3) **berdakosy** _____; Kevin Ray plays the (4) **sabs** _____; Sean Waugaman, the (5) **rumds** _____ and Eli Maiman, the (6) **tagiru** _____.

Grammar
Simple past – regular and irregular verbs (1): affirmative and negative

4 Complete the chart. Then circle the irregular verbs.

do	_did_	become	_____
_____	loved	have	_____
invent	_____	_____	finished
watch	_____	_____	went
_____	formed	perform	_____
_____	started		

5 Order the words to make sentences.

1. popular / in 1995 / cell / became / phones / .
   ___Cell phones became popular in 1995.___
2. band / didn't / the / yesterday / perform / .
   _____
3. ago / on vacation / Geoffrey / year / a / went / .
   _____
4. listen / Anna / didn't / to / music / night / last / .
   _____

6 Write true sentences about you. They can be affirmative or negative.

1. go to the movies / last week
   _____
2. go on vacation / last month
   _____
3. start school / in 2004
   _____
4. have breakfast / this morning
   _____
5. listen to music / last night
   _____
6. watch TV / yesterday morning
   _____

Vocabulary
TV shows

7 Find and circle eleven more kinds of TV shows in the spiral. What is your favorite?

8 Use words from Activity 7 to label the TV programmes.

1. *The Price Is Right* — game show
2. *CSI: Cyber* — _____
3. *The Simpsons* — _____
4. *Big Brother* — _____
5. *MTV Specials* — _____

9 Complete the words.

1. *The Babadook* is a really s<u>cary</u> movie. I suffered all the time.
2. My little sister doesn't like documentaries, but I find them i_____.
3. They showed *Cats the Musical* on TV last night. It was really f_____.
4. I loved *The Age of Adaline*, but my brother said it was b_____.
5. The news about the tornado in the USA is t_____.

Grammar
Be – simple past: affirmative and negative

10 Write the correct past form of *be* to complete the sentences. Use the affirmative (✔) or the negative (✘) form.

1. Michael Bublé __was__ great in the night show. (✔)
2. Last night's episode of my favorite series _____ really sad. (✔)
3. My friend Helen _____ at school yesterday. (✘)
4. Unfortunately, my teachers _____ interested in my story. (✘)
5. The actors in the school play _____ really fantastic! Everybody applauded a lot. (✔)
6. The movie _____ on Warner. It was on AXN at 10:00 p.m. (✘)

11 Write negative and affirmative sentences.

1. Rita / sad / yesterday (happy)
   Rita wasn't sad yesterday. She was happy.
2. My children / park / last weekend (movies)
   _____
3. Jane and Sarah / home / yesterday (sports center)
   _____
4. the movie / scary (funny)
   _____
5. last night's programe / interesting (boring)
   _____

12 Complete with the correct past form of *be*.

Jennifer and Alice are best friends. They usually walk to school and study all day long together. But yesterday (1) __was__ a different day. They didn't go to school. They traveled to Springfield with their parents. There (2) _____ a concert in a big stadium. It (3) _____ full of people. There (4) _____ more than six bands playing pop music. The money collected (5) _____ for charity. Fortunately, the weather (6) _____ good. The girls (7) _____ very happy.

Reading
A personal review

13 Read the text. Did the writer like the concert or not? _____

That concert was great!

Last Wednesday night, there was a wonderful concert at the local theater. The philharmonic orchestra and three choirs performed works by Bach, Mozart and Handel. It was really fantastic!

When the sounds of Mozart's *Ave Verum* for piano, violin, and choir started, the audience was in complete silence. That moment was magic. Classical music filled the theater and reached every corner of it.

The conductor of the orchestra was also a violin soloist. His solo was marvelous. We listened attentively to the performance. Violins, drums, trumpets, all instruments sounded wonderfully under the passionate direction of the conductor. And the invited pianist played her part really well!

They were celebrating the 79th anniversary of the town's foundation.

14 Read again and circle *T* (True) or *F* (False). Then correct the false sentences.

1. The concert was on the weekend.   T   F
   _____
2. There was one small choir.   T   F
   _____
3. The concert was in a soccer stadium.   T   F
   _____
4. There wasn't a piano in the orchestra.   T   F
   _____
5. The orchestra performed classical music.   T   F
   _____

15 Read again and answer the questions.

1. Where was the concert?
   _____
2. How many choirs were there?
   _____
3. Was the conductor good?
   _____
4. Was the writer in the audience?
   _____
5. Was there a celebration?
   _____

Speaking
Talking about likes and dislikes

16 Complete the conversation with the words from the box.

> Do you like   can't stand   I prefer
> do you like best   Let's
> Perfect   what about

Rick: (1) _____ organize the song playlist for the party.

Jenny: Good idea!

Rick: (2) _____ Rihanna?

Jenny: Yes, I love her!

Rick: What's your favorite song? How about *Where have you been*?

Jenny: No, (3) _____ *Don't stop the music*.

Rick: Great! I like that one too.

Jenny: And (4) _____ Beyoncé? Do you like her?

Rick: Oh, no. I (5) _____ her songs.

Jenny: Really? What else do you like?

Rick: I love David Guetta. He's so good.

Jenny: Well, I don't mind David Guetta. Which song (6) _____?

Rick: I really like *Titanium*. That's very popular.

Jenny: Great! And let's have something by Imagine Dragons, too..

Rick: Yes. How about *Radioactive*?

Jenny: (7) _____! OK. We're almost done!

Writing
A short biography

17 Read Jess Glynne's biography. Choose the correct options.

Jess Glynne

Jessica Hanna "Jess" Glynne is a British singer and songwriter. Her favorite types of music are R&B, soul and house. She doesn't play any instrument.

She wanted to compete in *The X Factor* when she (1) **is / was** 15, but they didn't accept her. Three years later, in 2008, she (2) **finished / finish** school, had different jobs, and traveled a lot.

The following year, she worked for a music company and (3) **does / did** a one-year course on music. In 2013, she participated in the album *Annie Mac Presents*. A year later, in January 2014, she (4) **become / became** famous when she was the vocalist with the electronic band Clean Bandit. They recorded a single and it (5) **were / was** number one on the UK Singles Chart; and it also got to top-five positions across Europe and Oceania.

The following month, in February 2014, Glynne uploaded a music video onto the Internet and she also appeared at several British music festivals.

In 2015, she became really famous and she launched her debut album: *I Cry When I Laugh*.

18 Complete the timeline about Jess Glyne.

2005:	2008:	2013:

2014: January: February:	2015:

19 Choose a celebrity you admire and write his/her biography in your notebook. Remember to include:

- country of origin
- early life
- details about his/her career
- when and why he/she became famous
- works and awards

UNIT 3 Fact or fiction?

Vocabulary
Types of books

1 Complete the sentences with the book titles from the box.

> The Adventures of Sherlock Holmes
> ~~Cooking: Fast and Easy~~   Visiting Europe
> Anne Frank's Diary (The Diary of a Young Girl)
> Churchill: A Life   The Martian
> The Complete Collected Poems of Maya Angelou

1 With _Cooking: Fast and Easy_, I can make cakes in 30 minutes.
2 I can't stop reading _____. An astronaut is on Mars. His spaceship breaks down and he can't return to Earth. It's fantastic!
3 "Phenomenal Woman" is a poem from _____. It defends women. I like it a lot.
4 I like reading _____. I always want to solve the cases with him.
5 I love learning about personalities in world history. I'm reading _____ at the moment.
6 I'm preparing my tour of Europe. I'm reading _____ for some help.
7 _____ is about a young girl during the Second World War. Her life was very hard.

2 Write the book titles from Activity 1 next to each type of book.

1 cookbook   _Cooking: Fast and Easy_
2 autobiography   _____
3 biography   _____
4 detective novel _____
5 poetry book   _____
6 science fiction novel _____
7 travel guide   _____

Grammar
Be – simple past: questions

3 Write questions. Then answer them.

1 Mark Twain / a famous writer? (✔)
   Was Mark Twain a famous writer? Yes, he was.
2 The Beatles / excellent musicians? (✔)
   _____
3 Mr. Patrick's classes / interesting and useful? (✔)
   _____
4 Tom and Helen / in Germany in 2011? (✘)
   _____
5 Christopher Columbus / American? (✘)
   _____

4 Complete with the correct past form of be. Then write questions about the text and answer them.

Hi! I'm Nicole. Last year, I (1) _was_ in Peru with my family. We (2) _____ on vacation. We (3) _____ there for a week. The weather (4) _____ fine almost every day. The mornings (5) _____ warm and the nights (6) _____ cool. I (7) _____ impressed by Machu Picchu. There (8) _____ a special atmosphere. The mountains (9) _____ magical. It (10) _____ an exciting and interesting experience.

1 Where / Nicole last year?
   Where was Nicole last year?
   She was in Peru.
2 Why / the family in Peru?
   _____
3 the weather / awful?
   _____
4 What / the mountains like?
   _____

Vocabulary
Verbs to talk about people's lives in the past

5 Find and circle nine more verbs in the simple past.

I	C	H	O	S	E	D	B
N	E	R	G	A	V	E	D
F	O	U	N	D	E	D	S
S	S	V	F	U	V	Q	O
P	A	W	D	I	E	D	L
E	W	K	I	L	L	E	D
N	O	P	E	N	E	D	J
T	H	O	U	G	H	T	E

6 Circle the correct options.
1. Malala Yousafzai **lived** / **thought** in Pakistan.
2. Walt Disney **decided** / **produced** many cartoons.
3. Nelson Mandela **enjoyed** / **thought** discrimination was wrong.
4. Steven Spielberg **made** / **had** his first *Jurassic Park* movie in 1993.
5. Mark Zuckerberg **wanted** / **created** Facebook some years ago.
6. Jessica Watson, the Australian sailor, **began** / **gave** a sailing trip around the world in 2009.
7. John Lennon **died** / **sold** in New York in December 1980.
8. Mandela and Lennon **wished** / **finished** to live in a world of peace.
9. A lot of people **wrote** / **bought** J.K. Rowling's books last year.

Grammar
Simple past – regular and irregular verbs (2): questions

7 Write the infinitive form of the verbs in Activities 5 and 6 in the correct column.

Regular verbs	Irregular verbs
	choose,

8 Write the simple past form of the verbs.

post ___posted___ love _____
go _____ write _____
download _____ buy _____
sell _____ start _____
earn _____ make _____

9 Complete the text about Emily with the correct past form of the verbs in parentheses. Then write questions about the text and answer them.

Last month, my mom (1) __gave__ (give) me *The Diary of a Wimpy Kid* for my birthday. I (2) _____ (begin) reading it one night and I never (3) _____ (stop) until I (4) _____ (finish) it.

Jeff Kinney (5) _____ (write) this book for younger kids, but I (6) _____ (enjoy) the stories very much because they (7) _____ (be) so funny!

Last week, I (8) _____ (go) to the new bookstore in town and (9) _____ (buy) other books in the series. I love every line I read!

1. Emily's mom / give / a sweater for her birthday?
   Did Emily's mom give her a sweater for her birthday?
   No, she didn't.
2. Who / write the *The Diary of a Wimpy Kid*?
   _____
3. Emily / like the book?
   _____
4. Why / Emily enjoy the stories?
   _____
5. Where / Emily buy other books in the series?
   _____

J.K. Rowling Nelson Mandela John Lennon

Reading
A timeline

10 Read the text and underline the regular past forms in green and the irregular past forms in red.

A BOOK THAT BECAME A MOVIE

Hans Christian Andersen was born in 1805 and <u>died</u> in 1875. He was Danish. He <u>wrote</u> many stories for children. One of his stories was *The Snow Queen*. It was a fairy tale and it appeared in many collections of illustrated books for children. It told the story of a fight between good and evil.

The story inspired different artists:

Josef Weinberger produced the musical play *The Snow Queen* in two acts.

San Jose Repertory Theatre produced a new musical adaptation called *The Snow Queen: A New Musical*. They received positive reviews.

1957 — 1969 — 2002 — 2005 — 2007 — 2013 →

Lev Atamanov directed a Soviet animated movie and Sandra Dee and Tommy Kirk gave their voices to the characters (Gerda and Kay).

David Wu directed a television movie for Hallmark, an American TV channel.

The British TV channel BBC adapted the story for television. They used computers for animations.

The English National Ballet premiered a three-act version of *The Snow Queen*.

Disney released the movie *Frozen*. They adapted the story for the movie and gave the protagonist a new name: Queen Elsa. The movie became a world hit.

11 Read again and correct the wrong information.

1 *The Snow Queen* is a historical novel.

_____

2 Shakespeare wrote the story.

_____

3 The story is about two lions and a girl.

_____

4 David Wu directed a musical for the theater.

_____

5 *Frozen* is a short book.

_____

12 Read again and answer the questions.

1 Did Hans Christian Andersen live in the 20th century?

_____

2 Was Hans an actor?

_____

3 When did the BBC adapt the story for television?

_____

4 Was there a ballet performance of *The Snow Queen*?

_____

Speaking
Talking about past events

13 Circle the correct options.

Mark: So, (1) **did / do** you have a good time in London on your last vacation?

Beth: Yes, thanks. It (2) **was / were** fantastic! We (3) **do / did** so many things! London is a great city!

Mark: I know the museums in London are very interesting. (4) **Did / Do** you visit any museums?

Beth: Yes, we (5) **do / did**! We went to Charles Dickens Museum. It was very (6) **exciting / boring**!

Mark: Really? (7) **Why / Who** was it so much fun?

Beth: We (8) **go / went** with a guide around the place. He was so (9) **funny / horrible**!

Mark: That sounds great! What part of the tour of the museum did you (10) **enjoy / enjoyed** most?

Beth: Well, I (11) **love / loved** hearing about Dickens's stories (12) **but / and** I also liked the manuscripts. We (13) **see / saw** many of his personal items, too.

Mark: It sounds exciting! I'm glad you enjoyed it. Tell me more about your visit...

Beth: Good idea! I'll tell you about it over lunch.

Writing
A review

14 Read the text and complete it with the phrases from the box.

> in the Maps Room
> and died in 1965 in London
> learned about the history of the Second World War, too
> I read Churchill's biography in *Churchill: A Life*
> We saw some of his possessions

Last Saturday, my family and I went to the Churchill War Rooms Museum in London. I enjoyed the visit because (1) _____. The museum was very interesting. We walked around the different rooms. We saw the maps and plans from the Second World War (2) _____.
We also visited Churchill's War Cabinet. (3) _____: his cap, his books, his clock…
For a moment, we lived in 1945!
Churchill was born in 1874, in Oxfordshire (4) _____. He was the Prime Minister of the United Kingdom. He was an army officer, a historian, a writer, and an artist.
I liked the museum store. It had nice souvenirs, but the prices were not cheap. I bought a small replica of Churchill's clock. We had a good time and (5) _____.

15 Choose a place you visited and write about it in your notebook. Remember to include:
- its name and location
- what you did
- what you liked / didn't like
- what you bought
- what the visit was like

UNIT 4 Life on Earth

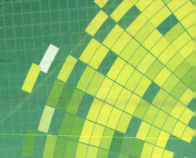

Vocabulary
Geographical features

1 Match the columns.

1	val	a	ert
2	water	b	ley
3	can	c	falls
4	des	d	ver
5	ri	e	forest
6	for	f	yon
7	isl	g	ke
8	ca	h	ach
9	oc	i	ve
10	rain	j	est
11	la	k	and
12	be	l	ean
13	re	m	ain
14	mount	n	ef

2 Complete the sentences with the correct form of the words from Activity 1.

1 Lake Como is a city in Italy. I like it because there are m<u>ountains</u> and beautiful l_____.
2 The Sahara is a big d_____ in Africa.
3 The Seine is a r_____ in Europe.
4 Most people love the warm b_____ in Aruba.
5 It rains a lot in the Amazon r_____. There are a lot of tropical plants in this area.
6 I learned that there are many tropical f_____ in Guatemala. They say they are beautiful.
7 Many tourists visit the Niagara w_____ every year. They are fantastic!
8 On Palancar Caves r_____ in Cozumel, there are a lot of c_____ and c_____.
9 The Bahamas is a group of i_____ in the Atlantic O_____.

Grammar
Adjectives: comparative and superlative forms

3 Complete the chart. Then circle the differences.

Adjective	Comparative	Superlative
long	long**er**	**the** long**est**
hot		
dry		
healthy		
beautiful		
good		
bad		
happy		
impressive		

4 Choose the correct options.

1 The Nile is **longer** / **the longest** river in the world. It is in Africa.
2 Beaches in the United States are **coldest** / **colder** than the beaches in the Caribbean.
3 Aconcagua is the **highest** / **higher** mountain in South America.
4 Deserts are **driest** / **drier** than rainforests.
5 Snorkelling is **more** / **most** unusual than swimming.

5 Complete with the correct form of the adjectives in parentheses.

New York is one of (1) <u>the most impressive</u> (impressive) cities in the world. There are many amazing places to visit.
All directions in New York use Central Park as a reference. That is (2) _____ (big) and (3) _____ (interesting) park in the city. There are many attractions there. You can walk through the park, but cycling can be (4) _____ (comfortable).
Visitors can take a cruise around Manhattan and see the Statue of Liberty. It is (5) _____ (old) and (6) _____ (tall) than the Eiffel Tower, in Paris and Christ the Redeemer, in Brazil.

Vocabulary
Environmental issues

6 Cross out three letters in each word and find the names of endangered species.

1. MOLNARICHE BLUTOTERFALIES — *monarch butterflies*
2. STERAS STLURTOLES ___
3. TRIGLERIS ___
4. MELEPAHANITS ___
5. SPOTLAIR BRETARES ___
6. SWHYACLES ___
7. GLORIALELAS ___
8. RACHINTOS ___
9. CAROLCODICLES ___
10. PRENAGLUINS ___

7 Write the names of animals from Activity 6 under each danger.

1. Ice platforms are melting.
   polar bears, …
2. Poachers hunt them.
   ___
3. They are losing their habitat.
   ___
4. People are cutting down trees.
   ___
5. Illegal hunters kill them for their tusks.
   ___
6. Tourists leave trash and disturb them.
   ___
7. Winters are colder and summers are hotter.
   ___
8. These animals can't find food.
   ___

Grammar
a / an, some, any, not much / many, a lot of, How much / many...?

8 Circle eight more countable nouns.

9 Write the plural forms of the countable nouns from Activity 8.

animals ___ ___
___ ___ ___
___ ___ ___

10 Circle the correct options.

1. There isn't **any** / **some** illegal hunting in our country.
2. Are there **any** / **some** colorful butterflies in the area?
3. There was **many** / **a lot of** clean water in the reserve.
4. We had **a** / **an** great time at the party yesterday.
5. They tried **any** / **some** traditional food when they were in Scotland.

11 Complete the questions with *How many* or *How much*. Then answer using the words in parentheses.

1. *How much* water is there in the lake? (a lot of)
   There is a lot of water in the lake.
2. ___ panda bears are there in the world? (many)
   ___
3. ___ rain is there in the rainforest? (a lot of)
   ___
4. ___ penguins are there in the desert? (any)
   ___

107

Reading
A TV interview

12 Read the interview. Then answer: What is the interview about? _____

I: Today, we're with James Greggson. He's a conservationist. Good evening, Mr. Greggson!
JG: Good evening, it's great to be here.
I: We want to know a bit more about your job. What do conservationists do?
JG: We protect endangered species.
I: Where do you work?
JG: I work for the World Wildlife Fund on the Galapagos Islands.
I: Oh, that's interesting! Do you have any good news to share?
JG: Yes. We're happy to say that the famous giant tortoise is not endangered anymore.
I: Were they really in danger of extinction?
JG: Oh, yes. A long time ago, in the 16th century, giant tortoises lived all over the world. In the 1960s, there were only four or five thousand. And in the 1970s, there were only 15 tortoises.
I: Oh! Why were they only 15?
JG: At the beginning, people hunted them and destroyed their habitat. Then, on the island, wild goats ate their food and damaged their habitat.
I: What did you do then?
JG: We took care of them in the reserve on Galapagos.

I: How many giant tortoises are there now?
JG: More than 1,000. And they are learning to survive in the wild.
I: Wow! What are they like?
JG: They are heavier than man. They can weigh 215 kg. They are the biggest tortoises in the world. They don't walk fast, but they can walk long distances. They eat grass, leaves and cactuses.
I: Do they live many years?
JG: One tortoise lived 170 years in captivity. I didn't look after her all that time! Haha!
I: Haha! That's amazing!

13 Read again and complete the timeline about Galapagos giant tortoises.

16th century	1960s	1970s	21st century
_____	_____	_____	_____

14 Read again and answer the questions.

1 Who is Mr. Greggson?
   _____

2 Why is he happy?
   _____

3 How many giant tortoises are there in the reserve?
   _____

4 Are the tortoises heavy?
   _____

5 Can they walk a lot?
   _____

6 What do the giant tortoises eat?
   _____

Speaking
Expressing preferences

15 Match the sentences 1–6 to the responses a–f. Underline the phrases that help to express preferences.

Zookeeper

1 Hello and welcome to our zoo. How can I help?

2 Great! Do you want to help the clerks in the zoo gift shop?

3 OK. How about cleaning the seals pool?

4 Yes, maybe that's a better idea for you. You can help zookeepers to feed the giraffes and the elephants.

5 No problem!

6 Yes, could you please fill in this form?

Margaret

a Thanks! That sounds more interesting than the other tasks.

b OK.

c Hello, I'd like to sign up for the volunteer day.

d Well, I don't mind cleaning, but I'm afraid of water. I prefer feeding the animals.

e That's good, but I'd rather do something with the animals.

f Do you need any details from me?

Writing
A travel guide article

16 Read the travel advice website. Identify the animals mentioned. Then answer: How many restaurants are there in the reserve?

_____

_____

www.beachesreserve.com

Friendly Beaches Reserve in Tasmania — a place to visit!

Do you want to experience nature? Come and visit us.
→ Stay at an unusual quiet wooden hotel in the middle of the forest.
→ Smell the relaxing fresh fragrant casuarinas and tea trees.
→ Sleep in comfortable, large, and modern beds.
→ Eat delicious fresh colorful fruit at the only local restaurant.
→ See collections of modern and ancient artworks from famous Tasmanian artists.
→ Walk along the amazing sugar-white sandy beaches.
→ See a lot of sea birds flying in the area (such as sea eagles, yellow-tailed cockatoos, bronze-winged pigeons, and more).
→ Don't miss the walking tour of Saltwater Lagoon and see the elegant black swans.
→ Take millions of photos!

17 Find and circle the adjectives in the text from Activity 16. Then classify them in the chart.

Opinion	
Size	
Age	
Color	
Material	
Other	

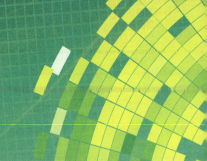

UNIT 5 Special days

Vocabulary
Celebrations

1 **Cross out two letters in each word and find words related to celebrations. Then use some of the words to complete the sentences.**

SPRIECIAL FOLCOD   CONTSTUMES
STREFEET ARPARADES   PAVERTY
RELATINAVES   HOKEUSE
PRESENORTS   FISTREWORKS
CAWSRDS   FUTEN

1 On New Year's Eve, my friends and I usually watch ___fireworks___ at midnight.
2 For Christmas, we eat _____ at home and then we visit _____.
3 Who decorates your _____ for special occasions?
4 My sister loves sending _____ to her friends for Christmas. I just send emails!
5 We sometimes wear _____ at school to celebrate Independence Day.
6 I love celebrating my birthday because I have a _____ and my friends give me _____. We have a lot of _____!

Grammar
Going to: affirmative, negative, and questions
Object pronouns

2 **Order the words to make sentences or questions.**

1 going / Dad / to / is / meat / cook / ?
   ___Is Dad going to cook meat?___
2 visit / on / to / am / I / friends / my / Saturday / going / not / .
   _____
3 grandparents / Costa Rica / to / travel / are / to / my / going / .
   _____

3 **Find three more questions and write them.**

Who	is	going	candy?	buy
How	Italy?	to	When	to
are	visit	cook?	are	going
they	to	going	you	he
going	to	travel?	Where	is

___Who is going to cook?___
_____
_____
_____

4 **Complete with the correct form of *going to* of the verbs in parentheses.**

Next Saturday, I (1) ___am going to celebrate___ (celebrate) my birthday. My friends (2) _____ (come) home in the afternoon. We (3) _____ (not be) more than five. Mom (4) _____ (make) a chocolate cake, my favorite. Fortunately, my sisters (5) _____ (not decorate) the house with balloons. That's for babies! My friends and I (6) _____ (play) my new video games. I am sure that we (7) _____ (have) a lot of fun.

5 **Circle the correct options.**

1 **I** / **Me** am talking to you, but you aren't listening to **I** / **me**.
2 Look at **she** / **her**. Everybody says **she** / **her** is cute.
3 I love One Direction. I listen to **they** / **them** every day before going to school.
4 There are some musicians at the square. Let's go and watch **they** / **them**.

110

Vocabulary
Adverbs of manner

6 Complete the chart. Then answer the questions.

	Adjective	Adverb
1	quick	quickly
2	hard	
3		loudly
4	nice	
5	healthy	
6		regularly
7	good	
8	easy	
9		dangerously
10	happy	
11		badly

a Underline in red the difference in "5," "8," and "10".
b What is different in "2" and "7"?

_____

7 Circle the correct options.

1 Look at Mom! She is smiling **loudly** / **happily** because my little brother is behaving **well** / **easily**.
2 Dad always works **badly** / **hard**. He loves his job.
3 I think I am not going to do **well** / **badly** in the race because I exercised **regularly** / **nicely**.
4 My sister usually speaks **healthily** / **loudly**.

Grammar
Present progressive for arrangements

8 Write *P* (Present) or *F* (Future).

1 My friend Peter is at home. He is singing loudly. __P__
2 We are preparing the school concert. _____
3 My best friend Alfred is coming to stay with us next week. _____
4 Are you and your family traveling to Europe in the summer? _____
5 When are the children playing soccer? _____

9 Look at Michael's diary notes and complete the text using the present progressive.

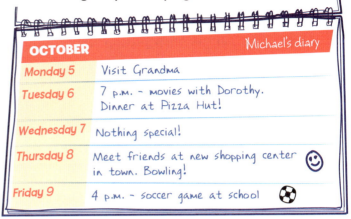

On Monday afternoon, I (1) _am visiting_ Grandma. On Tuesday evening, I (2) _____ with Dorothy and then we (3) _____ at Pizza Hut by the train station. Wednesday is my free day, so I (4) _____ . On Thursday, I (5) _____ my friends at the new shopping center in town. We (6) _____ , our favorite hobby. On Friday, I (7) _____ at school at 4.00 p.m. I hope we can win the match!

10 Write questions about the text from Activity 9. Then answer the questions.

1 What / Michael / do / on Monday?
   What is Michael doing on Monday?
   He's visiting his grandma.

2 Who / he / go / movies / with / on Tuesday?
   _____
   _____

3 Where / he / have / pizza?
   _____
   _____

4 Where / he / meet / friends / on Thursday?
   _____
   _____

5 What time / he / play / soccer / on Friday?
   _____
   _____

Reading
A tourist website

11 Read the website. Then answer: Which option do you prefer? _____

TWO GREAT OPTIONS!

BRAZIL IN JUNE
LEAVING ON JUNE 19th

We are taking you to Parintins. People celebrate the Parintins Folklore Festival there. It is one of the largest and most important festivals in Brazil. The festival takes place for three days at the end of June. Over 100,000 people participate in the festival. There is a competition in the *Bumbódromo* – a large spherical outdoor arena – between two teams: *Garantido* and *Caprichoso*.

Members of *Garantido* wear red clothes and members of *Caprichoso* wear blue clothes. You are going to watch parades and shows representing Amazonian folklore and indigenous culture. The teams dance and play traditional music. They also wear special costumes. You are going to have a lot of fun! We are going to have fun 24 hours a day.

The festival became world-wide famous when the musical group *Carrapicho* made **it** a hit in 1996.

ARGENTINA IN NOVEMBER
LEAVING ON NOVEMBER 8th

There is a famous celebration on November 10th in Argentina – Tradition Day – in honor of José Hernández, a well-known writer. His best-known work is the poem "*El Gaucho Martín Fierro*".

We are going to San Antonio de Areco. The celebration lasts a week there. People decorate houses, restaurants, and shops with Argentinian flags and traditional *gaucho* elements. Children wear costumes and dance *chacareras*, *zambas*, and the special *malambo*. People sing traditional folklore songs, and play the guitar and a drum called *bombo legüero* in special musical events called *peñas*.

Come and join us! You are going to have fun at the *peñas* and watch people parading on horseback. You are going to eat *asado* and *empanadas*. You are going to love **them**!

12 Read the website again and circle the correct options.

1 Parintins Folklore Festival takes place in **January / June**.
2 **Two / Three** teams compete in the festival.
3 You can **play / eat** *asado* and *empanadas* in San Antonio de Areco.
4 In both festivals, people wear colourful **costumes / customs**.

13 Read the website again and write *B* (Brazil), *A* (Argentina) or *BA* (Brazil and Argentina).

1 The festival lasts three days. ____
2 You are going to watch parades. ____
3 You can eat traditional food. ____
4 People wear red and blue clothes. ____
5 The celebration takes place when it is spring in the country. ____

14 Read again and complete the sentences.

1 There is a famous one-week celebration on _____ in San Antonio de Areco, in Argentina.
2 You are going to _____ parades and shows representing _____ culture.
3 In the first text, **"it"** refers to _____ and in the second one, **"them"** refers to _____.

112

Speaking
Making arrangements

15 Order Madison's lines and match them to Joshua's responses.

Madison

____ I'm going to the Mozart piano concert at the local theater. Do you want to come?

____ We're meeting in front of the theater at 8:00 p.m.

__1__ Hi, there. What are you up to?

____ Fantastic! See you on Friday.

____ My friend Katie and my cousin Ashley.

____ Listen, are you free on Friday?

Joshua

a Oh, nothing special. I'm going to my music class.

b Yes, I think so. Why?

c It sounds great! Who else is going?

d Good! What time are you going?

e Fine. Let's meet there.

f See you!

16 Read the conversation between Madison and Joshua again and answer the questions.

1 Do Madison and Joshua like music? How do you know?

_____

2 What kind of music are they going to listen on Friday evening?

_____

3 How many people are going to the concert with Madison?

_____

Writing
An invitation

17 Read the invitation and complete it with the correct prepositions.

Hello all!

We're celebrating "Happiness Day" (I invented it!) (1) _____ Saturday and we hope you can come!

The party is (2) _____ our house downtown on Saturday.
It starts (3) _____ 8:00 (4) _____ the evening.
I'm preparing sandwiches and juice. After that, Mom's serving ice cream.
We're going to listen to music and dance. We're going to wear funny costumes. Our friends from other schools are coming.

We're decorating the backyard with lots of balloons. Come and help us, please!

We're going to have lots of fun!

Grace

18 Invent a special day to celebrate and then write an invitation to your friends. List the details: *Where? When? What time? What activities? What food?* Use the invitation from Activity 17 as a model.

113

UNIT 6 Take care

Vocabulary
Physical and mental health

1 Match the columns.

1	exercise	a	your worries
2	discuss	b	regularly
3	don't get	c	about tests
4	don't get stressed	d	for yourself
5	eat	e	for help
6	try	f	into arguments
7	take time	g	your appearance
8	don't bully	h	a healthy diet
9	ask	i	other people
10	don't worry about	j	new sports

2 Complete the sentences.

1 Don't __get stressed__ about tests. Study thirty minutes every day and try to relax.

2 Teens _____ about their appearance all the time. That's stressing!

3 Teachers never _____ time for themselves. They need a break!

4 Do you want to get fit? _____ regularly.

5 Adults shouldn't _____ new sports without seeing a doctor.

6 Never _____ your classmates for help in tests. That's cheating!

7 Don't _____ new students in the class. Welcome them.

Grammar
Should: affirmative, negative, and questions

3 Order the words to make sentences or questions.

1 you / a / for / eat / light / should / dinner / snack / .
   __You should eat a light snack for dinner.__

2 shouldn't / about / children / their / worry / appearance / .
   _____

3 we / sports / should / practice / ?
   _____

4 bully / teenagers / classmates / their / shouldn't / .
   _____

5 for / we / ask / help / should / .
   _____

4 Write pieces of advice. Then write sentences "2", "4", and "6" as questions.

1 sleep 8 hours a day
   __You should sleep 8 hours a day.__

2 play video games all day long
   _____

3 exercise one hour a day
   _____

4 work in groups
   _____

5 help your classmates
   _____

6 eat fast food every day
   _____

114

Vocabulary
Health problems and first aid

5 Find and circle ten more words that describe health problems and first aid.

C	K	B	L	I	S	T	E	R	S	M	I
L	O	A	J	K	F	Z	X	K	U	A	Q
A	N	T	A	C	I	D	R	T	N	S	U
S	N	Y	I	T	C	O	L	D	B	P	I
J	B	A	L	T	R	F	P	G	U	I	B
E	G	C	V	O	E	G	I	I	R	R	A
R	H	E	A	D	A	C	H	E	N	I	C
S	P	A	J	A	M	H	E	A	E	N	K
B	I	T	E	S	W	E	R	N	M	S	A
S	U	N	S	C	R	E	E	N	I	O	C
W	L	S	A	O	L	R	Y	I	L	I	H
T	S	T	O	M	A	C	H	A	C	H	E

6 Complete the sentences with words from Activity 5.

1 Mary has a terrible h<u>eadache</u>. She should stop using the computer.
2 Henry ate a lot of chocolate. He has a s_____.
3 Are you going trekking? Well, take some adhesive bandages in case you get b_____ on your feet.
4 I carried a really heavy backpack for two hours. Now, I have b_____.
5 Before leaving, check that you have some a_____ in your first aid kit.
6 Sophie has a c_____. She should stay in bed and take some medicine.

Grammar
The infinitive of purpose

7 Match the columns. Then choose a verb from box A and a phrase from box B and write pieces of advice.

1 Buy clothes — a Twitter
2 You should join — b on vacation
3 Why don't you go — c comfortable shoes
4 Try to wear — d fruit and vegetables
5 Children should eat — e exercise regularly
6 We should — f at the end of the season

A be   climb   contact   ~~get~~   keep   relax

B healthy   friends   ~~cheaper prices~~   on the beach   the mountain   fit

1 <u>Buy clothes at the end of the season to get cheaper prices.</u>
2 _____
3 _____
4 _____
5 _____
6 _____

8 Write questions. Then complete the answers.

1 Why / for tests / we / study?
<u>Why should we study for tests?</u>
<u>To pass</u> _____ the tests.
2 Why / babies / use special sun cream?
_____
_____ their skin.
3 Why / you / take some antacid?
_____
_____ better.
4 Why / people / take money on the trip?
_____
_____ the tickets to the show.
5 Why / we / take an adhesive bandage?
_____
_____ on blisters.

Reading
A tourists' forum

9 Read the answers in the forum. Then write the questions from the box in the correct place.

> Are there good beaches in the area?   Do I need a passport and a visa to go there?
> What about cultural attractions?   What places can I visit?   Can I use my credit card?

VALPARAÍSO: The Jewel of the Pacific

Planning to travel this summer? Think about visiting Valparaíso! You are going to love it!
Do you have any queries? Join this tourists' forum to find out.

1 _____
You have to check the requirements to enter the country. Most of the times, an ID is OK, but you should take it everywhere.

2 _____
Yes, you can use it at hotels, restaurants, and big stores. But you should bring Chilean money (*pesos*) to buy candy, chewing gum, or small souvenirs from small stores.

3 _____
Yes, they are really nice! But you should bring sunscreen to protect your skin. And you should be careful with children because the sea water can be very cold. Bring some warm clothes, too.

4 _____
You shouldn't miss the view of the city from the mountains. There are funiculars that take people up and down the 45 mounts that surround the city. It is like a natural amphitheater! You are going to see the colors of the city from the top. You should also visit Prat Pier to see the small fishing boats. There are also bigger ships.

5 _____
Visiting *La Sebastiana* is a must! Pablo Neruda, the famous poet, lived there. It has a wonderful view of the sea from all its windows.

You should appreciate all the city's historical architecture, traditions, and art. UNESCO included Valparaíso's historical area on the list of World Heritage Sites in 2003.

10 Read the forum again and check (✔) what you should take to Valparaíso.

1. chewing gum ☐   4. warm clothes ☐
2. sunscreen ☐   5. cold water ☐
3. dollars ☐

11 Read the forum again and correct the wrong information.

1. There are no questions in the forum.
_____

2. You can only use credit cards in big shops.
_____

3. The sea water is always warm.
_____

4. *La Sebastiana* is a new restaurant near the beach.
_____

5. UNESCO is going to include Valparaíso's historical area on the list of World Heritage Sites.
_____

Speaking
Talking about health

12 Complete the conversation with words or phrases from the box.

> appointment   help you   get well
> much is it   put   the matter
> worse   You should take

At the drugstore…
Clerk: Hi! Can I (1) _____?
Customer: Yes. I need your advice.
Clerk: What's (2) _____?
Customer: I have a terrible backache!
Clerk: Oh, no! What happened?
Customer: I carried my little son on my shoulders for an hour. We went to Pinocchio's Show.
Clerk: (3) _____ some aspirins and (4) _____ this cream on your back.
Customer: OK. How many aspirins should I take?
Clerk: Just one after lunch and one after dinner.
Customer: All right.
Clerk: And you should make a doctor's (5) _____ if the backache gets (6) _____.
Customer: OK, I will. How (7) _____?
Clerk: $6.
Customer: Here you are.
Clerk: I hope you (8) _____ soon!
Customer: Thanks. Bye!

Writing
Emails

13 Order the lines 1–8 to organize Alice's email.

To: Rachel
From: Alice

a ___ Mom thinks I should stay at home, but I don't want to miss tonight's show.
b ___ How are you?
c ___ Alice
d ___ I want to go to the disco tonight but I have a terrible headache.
e ___ My favorite group, Five Attack, are performing!
f _1_ Hi, Aldana!
g ___ I'm writing to you because I want some advice.
h ___ What should I do?

14 Write Rachel's reply. Use *should* to give advice and phrases from the box.

> Sorry you are not well.   I think you…
> Last week, I had a headache and…
> I hope I can help!   Good luck!

To: Alice
From: Rachel

_____
_____
_____
_____

Consolidation

1 Complete the text with the correct form of the verbs in parentheses. Use the present progressive, the simple present, the simple past, or *-ing* forms.

Ben Wilson, the chewing gum man

Look at the man in the picture. What (1) _____ (he / do)? (2) _____ (he / paint) the sidewalk? No, he isn't. What is he painting then? He (3) _____ (paint) a piece of chewing gum on the sidewalk! Read to find out about his art.

This man is Ben Wilson. He is a British artist. He (4) _____ (live) with his family in London.

Ben (5) _____ (be born) in Cambridge, in 1963. When he (6) _____ (be) a child, he (7) _____ (live) in Barnet. When he (8) _____ (finish) school, he (9) _____ (go) to art college, but he (10) _____ (not finish) his studies.

When Ben (11) _____ (be) about 35 years old, he (12) _____ (have) an idea and he (13) _____ (invent) a new form of art: miniature paintings on chewing gum! Today, there are about 10,000 gum paintings by him in London and other areas of Europe. The majority of his paintings (14) _____ (be) in Muswell Hill.

Ben (15) _____ (make) his first gum paintings in 1998. He (16) _____ (begin) working full-time on this form of art in 2004 and he (17) _____ (become) famous in his community. In 2009, when the police arrested him for painting graffiti in London, the local people (18) _____ (help) him. They (19) _____ (write) letters to the police because they (20) _____ (like) his art. "My art (21) _____ (not be) graffiti because I never (22) _____ (paint) the sidewalk. I always (23) _____ (paint) the gum," Ben says.

Sometimes, people ask him to paint things for them and he (24) _____ (do) his work for free! He likes (25) _____ (travel) around London and (26) _____ (listen) to people. People enjoy (27) _____ (watch) him when he is working. "My work (28) _____ (not be) boring. It (29) _____ (be) about people and their lives," he says.

Ben also (30) _____ (make) normal paintings and wood sculptures. There are documentaries about him because he (31) _____ (be) a very interesting man.

2 Correct the sentences. Write a negative and an affirmative sentence.

1 In the picture, Ben is making a sculpture.

_____

2 Ben and his family live in Barnet.

_____

3 Ben invented a new form of music.

_____

4 The local people were happy when the police arrested him.

_____

3 Complete the conversation with the simple past form of the verbs in parentheses.

James: What (1) _____ (you / watch) on TV last night?

Wendy: I (2) _____ (watch) a documentary about Ben Wilson.

James: Ben Wilson? Who's that?

Wendy: A British artist. He paints chewing gum stuck on the sidewalk.

James: Really? (3) _____ (the documentary / be) interesting?

Wendy: Yes, it (4) _____ (be). It (5) _____ (be) very interesting. And what (6) _____ (you / do) last night?

James: I (7) _____ (go) to the movies. I (8) _____ (see) a nice comedy.

Wendy: It sounds great.

118

Project

A timeline

Let's analyze.

1 Read the definition and look at the timeline.

> **timeline:** a tool to show a series of events in order. You can use a timeline to give information about the life of a person or important events in history.

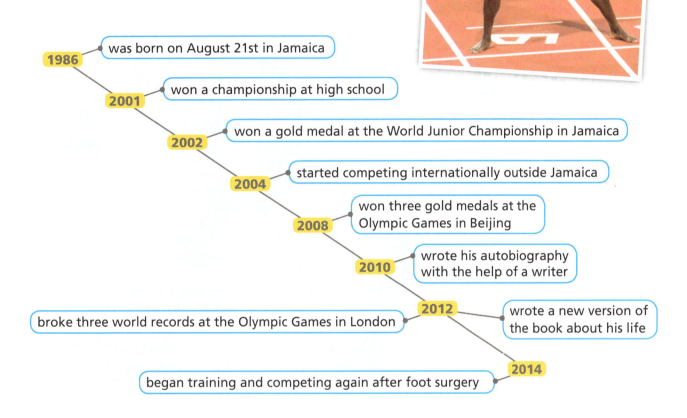

- 1986 — was born on August 21st in Jamaica
- 2001 — won a championship at high school
- 2002 — won a gold medal at the World Junior Championship in Jamaica
- 2004 — started competing internationally outside Jamaica
- 2008 — won three gold medals at the Olympic Games in Beijing
- 2010 — wrote his autobiography with the help of a writer
- 2012 — broke three world records at the Olympic Games in London; wrote a new version of the book about his life
- 2014 — began training and competing again after foot surgery

Let's do it!

Step 1 Sit in groups of three or four students. Choose a famous sportsperson, artist, musician, or writer and create a timeline about his/her life. Go online and find his/her date of birth and the important events in his/her life. You can use the following search terms: *biography of [person's name]*.

Step 2 Organize the information on the Project Planning sheet. Remember to use vocabulary and structures from Units 1, 2, and 3.

Step 3 Make your timeline. Choose one of these options:

- Go online and search for a timeline creator. Complete the timeline with the information about the famous person you chose. If possible, add images or videos to make it more interesting.
- Make a poster using the timeline in Activity 1 as a model.

Step 4 Share your work.

- If you used an online timeline creator, share the link with your teacher and your class.
- If you created a poster, show it to your class and read the information aloud.

119

Consolidation

1 Circle the correct options.

ARCTIC ADVENTURE

Do you want to try something different? Come on an Arctic survival vacation in the Taiga!

The Taiga is (1) **a / an** area that covers the northern part of North America, Europe and Asia. It is home to the (2) **larger / largest** forest in the world. There are (3) **much / a lot of** wild animals and the landscape is beautiful. There are tall trees and (4) **some / any** nice lakes and waterfalls. But the Taiga is (5) **dangerously / dangerous**, too. There aren't (6) **many / much** people in the area (7) **for / to** help you in case of a problem. On our Arctic Adventure, our instructors teach you the skills you need (8) **surviving / to survive**.

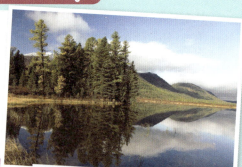

TIPS AND COMMENTS

It's really wonderful here. We're staying in small cabins. They are comfortable, but there isn't (9) **an / any** electricity. Our instructor is teaching (10) **our / us** many survival skills. We don't have (11) **much / many** food. Tomorrow, we (12) **'re leaving / leave** early in the morning. We (13) **'re going / go** to a lake to catch (14) **any / some** fish for lunch. *Randall*

In some areas of the Taiga, people are cutting down trees (15) **building / to build** roads and houses, and animals are losing their habitat. I think governments should (16) **create / to create** national parks (17) **protect / to protect** wildlife. *Vincent*

The Taiga is large and dangerous. You (18) **should / shouldn't** explore the area on your own because you can get lost (19) **easily / easy**. You should travel with an instructor. They know the area (20) **good / well**. *Sean*

The (21) **better / best** time to visit the Taiga is in the summer. In the summer, temperatures are (22) **the highest / higher than** in the winter, but they're still cold – about 10ºC. You should pack a jacket and warm clothes. You're going to need (23) **they / them**! *Lina*

You (24) **'re doing / 're going to do** a lot of walking, so pack some adhesive bandages. I didn't pack (25) **much / any** and I got blisters on my feet! *Greg*

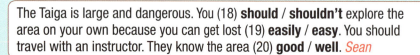

2 Correct the sentences. Write a negative and an affirmative sentence.

1. You should pack summer clothes.
   _____
2. Randall is climbing a mountain tomorrow.
   _____
3. On a trip to the Taiga, you are going to do a lot of swimming.
   _____
4. People are cutting down trees to build cities.
   _____

3 Order the words to make questions. Then answer.

1. any / electricity / the / is / there / cabins / in / ?
   _____
   _____
2. animals / are / area / wild / there / the / any / in / ?
   _____
   _____
3. snow / there / much / these / forests / how / is / in ?
   _____
   _____

Project

A general knowledge quiz

Let's analyze.

1 Read the definition and look at the quiz.

> **general knowledge quiz:** a questionnaire that includes questions on animals, places, science, history, and famous people. When you do an online quiz, you can see the answers immediately.

2 Read the quiz and answer these questions.
   1 What is the title of the quiz?
     _____
   2 Which are the correct answers? Circle them in the quiz.
   3 Can you think of three questions to add to the quiz? Write them below.

ANIMAL QUIZ

1 The fastest animal on the planet is the ... .
  a lion   b horse
  c cheetah   d tiger

2 Poachers kill elephants for their ... .
  a horn   b skin
  c teeth   d tusks

3 Polar bears hunt for food ... .
  a in forests   b from ice platforms
  c on beaches   d in mountains

_____
_____
_____
_____
_____

Let's do it!

Step 1 Sit in groups of three or four students. Look at the list below and choose a topic for your quiz. Then go online and find information about the topic you chose.

- Impressive places on Earth
- Amazing animals
- Festivals and celebrations around the world
- Adventure travel: tips and interesting information

Step 2 Organize the questions and answers on the Project Planning sheet. Don't make your quiz too difficult. Remember to use vocabulary and structures from Units 4, 5, and 6.

Step 3 Choose one of these options:

- Go online and search for a quiz-making tool. Input your questions and answers.
- Make a quiz on a sheet of paper using the quiz in Activity 2 as a model. Add some images to make it more attractive.

Step 4 Share your work.

- If you used an online quiz-making tool, share the link with your teacher and your class.
- If you created a quiz on paper, make photocopies and hand them out to your classmates.

121

creative corner

What is the "fantastic" in literature

The "fantastic" is any part of a story that confuses the reader about whether the story can be real or supernatural.

1 Read the stories and circle the words that frighten you in each story.

What are two-sentence stories?

They are stories that people write – usually on the Internet – that have a maximum of two sentences. There are many websites with this type of stories.

a It's 10:00 p.m. and I give my little daughter a goodnight kiss[1] when she says, "Daddy, there's a monster under my bed." I look under the bed and I see her looking at me frightened[2] and saying, "Daddy there's somebody on my bed."

b It was 6:00 a.m. and my wife was already downstairs, making her usual noise in the kitchen. As I turned in bed, I could see her, still sleeping next to me.

c I reached[3] for the remote control to change channels. It felt strange as there was another hand on it in my empty bedroom.

d "Daddy, Daddy, my robot is going round and round and saying he will destroy you," shouted the little boy in his bedroom. But his weak father, trapped in the basement[4], couldn't hear him.

e It was a stormy[5] night. I walked sleepily into the bathroom and looked at myself in the mirror, but only one of us walked out.

2 Read the stories again and complete the sentences.

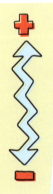

The most (+) frightening is story ☐ because _____ _____ _____.

The least (–) frightening is story ☐ because _____ _____ _____.

Glossary

1 kiss

2 frightened: scared

3 to reach: to move your hand to something

4 basement

5 stormy

122

3 Read the stories again and write a title for each of them.

a _____

b _____

c _____

d _____

e _____

4 Choose one of the stories and write one more sentence.

_____

_____

_____

_____

_____

5 Choose one of the stories. Imagine it is the blurb of a book (brief description you find on the back cover). Write the book title, author's name, blurb and author's biography. Draw the front cover and author's picture. Use vocabulary from Unit 3.

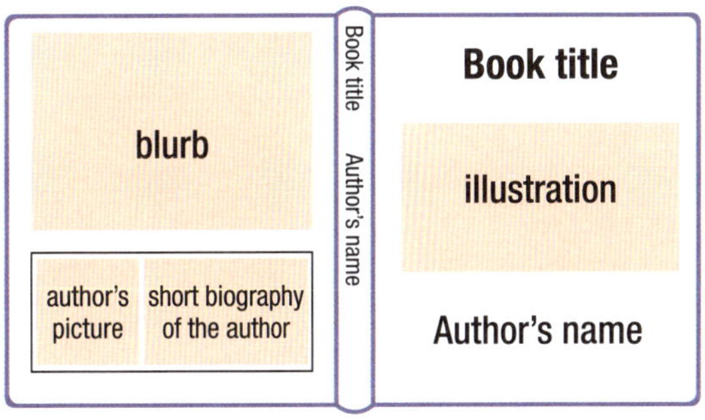

blurb

author's picture | short biography of the author

Book title

Author's name

Book title

illustration

Author's name

Fantastic two-sentence stories

123

Adventure story

What is an adventure story?

It is a story in which the main elements are action and courageous characters that save others from danger. This kind of story is usually centered on a protagonist in a dangerous or risky situation.

Robinson Crusoe
by Daniel Defoe

Daniel Defoe was an English journalist and writer. Defoe's inspiration for *Robinson Crusoe* was probably the story of a Scottish castaway[1] called Alexander Selkirk. Selkirk, a Scottish sailor, was rescued in 1709 after living for four years on the uninhabited island of Más a Tierra, now called Robinson Crusoe Island, in the Juan Fernández Islands off the Chilean coast.

Robinson Crusoe belongs to a traditional family. His father encourages him to study Law. Instead, he goes to sea with a friend. This first travel proves financially successful. On a second sea travel leaving London, Robinson is enslaved by Moorish pirates and he is taken to Africa first and then to Brazil. In Brazil, Robinson becomes the owner of a plantation. As he needs slaves[2], he travels again to Africa.

In the Atlantic Ocean, there is a terrible storm with a hurricane[3] and the crew decide to get in a lifeboat[4]. Unfortunately, the lifeboat capsizes[5] in the rough sea and Robinson is the only one who saves his life because he manages to reach[6] an island. "I'm so lucky," Robinson thinks. "I'm the only one who knew to swim well."

Robinson decides to build a place where to live. He calls it a "fortress." From this place, he can see the sea and he is also protected from animals.

One day, the ship in which he was sailing, gets closer to the island. Robinson sees the ship and starts making a raft[7].

"I want to go to the ship to see what I can get," he thinks.

After six voyages, Robinson brings knives[8], food, seeds, clothes, tools, nails, some money, a hammock[9], blankets, pistols and, of course, gunpowder.

Unfortunately, one day there is a terrible storm and the ship is destroyed. Robinson thinks, "I'll get the wood. I need it."

On one of his voyages to the ruined ship, Robinson rescues a dog and two cats, along with ink and pens, and a Bible. He starts reading the Bible at night. Then he proclaims himself king of the island.

One day, Robinson is walking along the beach. There, he can see some footprints[10], so he gets surprised and worried. "Oh no!" he thinks. "I know these are cannibals" footprints! They live in the area."

Robinson is on the alert now. He is armed and builds an underground house.

Adventure story

Adventure story

One Friday morning, he sees about thirty cannibals with a victim.
"Cannibals!" he thinks. "I believe they want to kill that man. I'll save him!"

Suddenly, Robinson shoots at the cannibals and saves their victim. The young man is grateful[11] to Robinson. Robinson calls him Friday. He teaches Friday to speak English and encourages him to eat goat[12].

Glossary

1 **castaway**: a person who escaped from a sunken ship and is now on an island with few or no people

2 **slave**: a person who belongs to another person and has to work for them

3 **hurricane**: violent wind

4 **lifeboat**: a small boat on a ship for people to leave in if the ship is not safe

5 **to capsize**: to turn upside down in the water

6 **"manages to reach"**: "makes an effort to get to"

7 raft

8 knife (pl. knives)

9 hammock

10 footprints

11 **grateful**: showing or expressing thanks

12 goat

---

1 Imagine you are Robinson Crusoe. You are back home. You are now with a journalist. He wants to know about your life on the island. Complete the conversation.

Journalist: What did you do before going to the island?
Robinson: (1) _____

Journalist: How did you get to the island?
Robinson: (2) _____

Journalist: What did you take with you from the ship?
Robinson: (3) _____

Journalist: How did you get food?
Robinson: (4) _____

Journalist: How did you make your wooden house?
Robinson: (5) _____

2 Imagine you are Friday. Write a blog post in your notebook. Tell your followers why the cannibals captured you, how Robinson Crusoe rescued you and whether you liked Robinson or not.

3 Robinsonade is a genre created after the success of the 1719 novel *Robinson Crusoe* by Daniel Defoe. It is sometimes described simply as a "desert island story". Read and match the Robinsonades' titles with the story summaries.

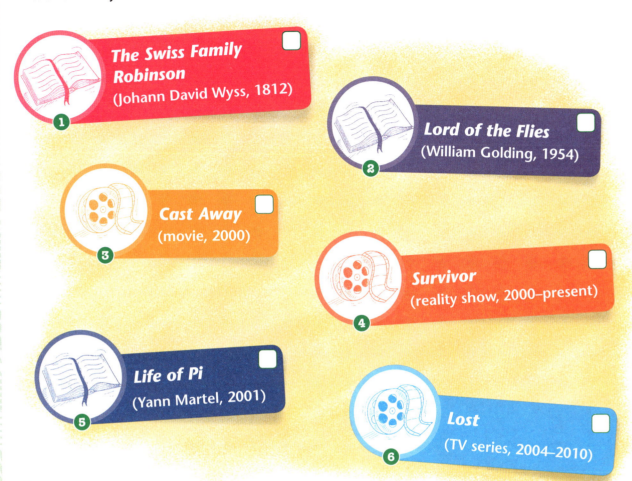

1. *The Swiss Family Robinson* (Johann David Wyss, 1812)
2. *Lord of the Flies* (William Golding, 1954)
3. *Cast Away* (movie, 2000)
4. *Survivor* (reality show, 2000–present)
5. *Life of Pi* (Yann Martel, 2001)
6. *Lost* (TV series, 2004–2010)

a. These castaways compete for money and other prizes. They eliminate each other until one of them is the only one left on the island.

b. These castaways live on a mysterious tropical island in the Pacific after their plane flying between Sydney and Los Angeles crashes.

c. This young castaway lives on a lifeboat in the Pacific Ocean with a Bengal tiger after his ship sinks together with his whole family.

d. The crew of the ship abandons these castaways after it crashes against a reef. They decide to make the island they find beyond the reef their new home and take food and two dogs together with them.

e. This castaway works for FedEx and his plane crashes in the South Pacific. He survives on an island using the cargo they were going to deliver.

f. In the middle of the war, a plane that is evacuating a group of schoolboys is shot and crashes against a tropical island where only the children survive as castaways.

Romeo and Juliet

Romeo and Juliet come from enemy families, the Montagues and the Capulets. They meet at a party by chance and fall in love. Now Romeo is in the Capulet's garden because he wants to see Juliet once again.

Juliet is in her balcony. She looks sad. She doesn't know that Romeo is in her garden, watching her. So she speaks to herself.

Juliet: Ah!
Romeo: She speaks! Oh, speak again, angel!
Juliet: Oh, Romeo, Romeo! Where are you? Why is your name Romeo? Say you don't want your father and your name. Forget about your family and change your name. If you don't, I will not be a Capulet any longer.
Romeo: What can I do? Hear or speak?
Juliet: It is only your name that is my enemy. What is a name? When we use another name to call a rose, it still smells sweet. If Romeo is no longer Romeo, he will still be perfect.
Romeo: I hate my name because it is your enemy.

Juliet sees Romeo and she looks surprised. Now they start talking.

Juliet: Who is there? I heard very few words from you, but I know the sound of your voice. Are you Romeo and a Montague?
Romeo: I am not Romeo and I am not a Montague if you hate both.
Juliet: My family will kill you if they see you here!
Romeo: The night is hiding me. And if you don't love me, I want them to find me here. My life can finish with their hate because it can't continue without your love.
Juliet: Who is helping you?
Romeo: Love guides me. I will go anywhere to find you.
Juliet: Do you love me? Oh, good Romeo. If you love me, please say it.
Romeo: Lady, I swear by the moon.
Juliet: Do not swear by the inconstant moon.
Romeo: What can I swear by?
Juliet: Do not swear. Everything is happening very fast. If you want to marry me, please send me a message tomorrow. And I will come to you and my future is yours.

Romeo and Juliet kiss. They are really happy.

1 Read and rewrite Romeo's messages.

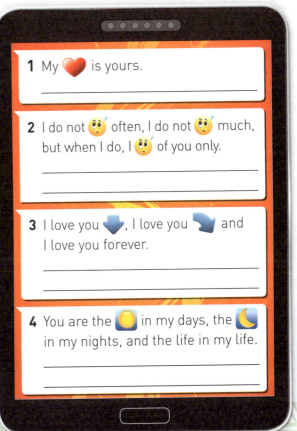

1 My ♥ is yours.
_____

2 I do not 😢 often, I do not 😢 much, but when I do, I 😢 of you only.
_____
_____

3 I love you ⬇, I love you ↩ and I love you forever.
_____
_____

4 You are the ☀ in my days, the 🌙 in my nights, and the life in my life.
_____
_____

Romeo and Juliet

129

2 Imagine you are Juliet at the end of the day she met Romeo. Complete your blog with the correct simple past form of the verbs in parentheses

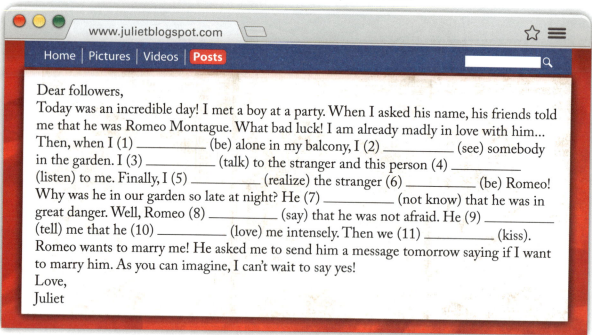

Dear followers,
Today was an incredible day! I met a boy at a party. When I asked his name, his friends told me that he was Romeo Montague. What bad luck! I am already madly in love with him... Then, when I (1) _____ (be) alone in my balcony, I (2) _____ (see) somebody in the garden. I (3) _____ (talk) to the stranger and this person (4) _____ (listen) to me. Finally, I (5) _____ (realize) the stranger (6) _____ (be) Romeo! Why was he in our garden so late at night? He (7) _____ (not know) that he was in great danger. Well, Romeo (8) _____ (say) that he was not afraid. He (9) _____ (tell) me that he (10) _____ (love) me intensely. Then we (11) _____ (kiss). Romeo wants to marry me! He asked me to send him a message tomorrow saying if I want to marry him. As you can imagine, I can't wait to say yes!
Love,
Juliet

3 Imagine you are Romeo. Write a message to Juliet asking her to marry you in secret and saying when and where you both are going to marry. Include any love sentence from Activity 1.

4 Imagine Juliet's father appears when Juliet and Romeo are talking in the garden. Create three scenes. Use captions and speech bubbles.

1 What does her father say to them?

2 What do Romeo and Juliet say to him?

3 What happens then?

Student A

UNIT 1

1 Answer about you. Then interview Student B and write his/her answers in the second column.

Do you...	You	Student B
sometimes cook dinner?		
hang out with friends on Fridays?		
chat online every day?		
listen to music when you do your homework?		

2 Answer Student B's questions. Compare your answers. Are your habits and likes similar?

UNIT 2

1 Look at the chart and describe Tom's vacation to confirm the information. Student B corrects the information when necessary.

	Facts to confirm	True facts
Destination	Spain	
People	with uncle, aunt, and four cousins	
Duration	3 weeks	
Accommodation	hotel near downtown	

🟠 *Tom was on vacation in Spain.*

2 Read about Sally's vacation. Listen to Student B and correct the information when necessary.

Last year, Sally was on vacation with her family in France. She was with her mom and dad, and her brother James. They were there for five days. They were in a small hotel near the Eiffel Tower.

UNIT 3

1 Find out if the underlined information is true. Correct the mistakes orally.

Ellen MacArthur was born in 1986. She started sailing when she was 4. She liked reading biographies. When she was 8, she decided to buy a bicycle. She bought her first boat when she was 13.

🟠 *Was Ellen MacArthur born in 1986?*

2 Look at the chart and answer Student B's questions.

Charles Darwin	
1809	was born
1827–1831	studied at university, liked collecting insects (beetles)
1831	started a sailing trip to the southern hemisphere
1859	wrote his book *The Origin of Species*

UNIT 4

1 Read about Iberian lynxes and answer Student B's questions.

Description of Iberian lynxes: they are wild cats; they eat meat; they live in Spain; they can live for 13 years.
Reasons why they are in danger: they can't find enough food; people kill them.

2 Ask questions to find out about loggerhead turtles and complete the file.

🟠 *Where do loggerhead turtles live?*

Loggerhead turtles	
Live in?	
Food	
Life span	
In danger? Why?	

UNIT 5

1 Design a celebration. Make notes in your notebook to answer: What type of celebration (a house party, a beach party, a music festival, a picnic)? Where? When? Who are you going to invite? What activities are you going to do?

2 Ask questions to find out about Student B's celebration. Then answer his/her questions.

🟠 *Are you going to have a house party?*

UNIT 6

1 You're going on a trip to Andalucía in Spain. Ask questions to complete the tips.

🟠 *What should I buy in advance? Why?*

A trip to Andalucía
- You should buy (1) _____ in advance to (2) _____ .
- You should use (3) _____ on the beach because temperatures can reach 45°C in the summer.
- You shouldn't go shopping at (4) _____ because (5) _____ .

2 Read the tips and answer Student B's questions.
Tips for climbing Mount Kilimanjaro
- Go with a guide because you can get lost.
- Take water. You should drink 3 liters per day.
- Exercise regularly before you go, so you have the right training.
- Don't climb quickly. Go slowly to help your body feel better.

131

Student B

UNIT 1

1 Answer about you. Then answer Student A's questions.

Do you...	You	Student A
ride your bike on weekends?		
usually watch videos on YouTube?		
sometimes go for a run?		
like painting?		

2 Interview your classmate and write his/her answers in the second column. Compare your answers. Are your habits and likes similar?

UNIT 2

1 Read about Tom's vacation. Listen to Student A and correct the information when necessary.

This time last year, Tom was on vacation in Brazil. He was with his uncle and aunt, and his cousin. They were in a small house near the beach. They were there for two weeks.

2 Look at the chart and describe Sally's vacation to confirm the information. Your classmate corrects the information when necessary.

	Facts to confirm	True facts
Destination	the USA	
People	mother, father, and sister Janet	
Duration	10 days	
Accommodation	house near beach	

💬 *Sally was on vacation in the USA.*

UNIT 3

1 Look at the chart and answer Student A's questions.

Ellen MacArthur	
1976	was born
4 years old	started sailing
	liked reading books about sailing
8 years old	decided to buy a boat
13 years old	bought her first boat

2 Find out if the underlined information is true. Correct the mistakes orally.

Charles Darwin was born <u>in 1809</u>. When he was 18 years old, he started his studies at university. He had an interesting hobby – he liked <u>collecting flowers</u>! In 1831, he started a sailing trip to the Arctic. In 1859, he wrote his famous book *The Origin of Species*.

💬 *Was Charles Darwin born in 1809?*

UNIT 4

1 Ask questions to find out about Iberian lynxes and complete the file.

💬 *Where do Iberian lynxes live?*

Iberian lynxes	
Live in?	
Food	
Life span	
In danger? Why?	

2 Read about loggerhead turtles and answer Student A's questions.

Description of loggerhead turtles: they live in the Atlantic, Pacific, and Indian Oceans, and in the Mediterranean Sea; they can live for 67 years; they eat plants and fish.

Reasons why they are in danger: they die in fishing nets; people kill them for their shells and eggs.

UNIT 5

1 Design a celebration. Make notes in your notebook to answer: What type of celebration (a house party, a beach party, a music festival, a picnic)? Where? When? Who are you going to invite? What activities are you going to do?

2 Answer Student A's questions. Then ask questions to find out about his/her celebration.

💬 *No, I'm not going to have a house party.*

UNIT 6

1 Read the tips and answer Student A's questions.
Tips for a trip to Andalucía in Spain
* You should buy train tickets in advance to find special offers.
* You should use sunscreen on the beach because temperatures can reach 45°C in summer.
* You shouldn't go shopping at midday because shops are closed.

2 You're planning to climb Mount Kilimanjaro. Ask questions to complete the tips.

💬 *Who should I go with? Why?*
Climbing Mount Kilimanjaro
* Go with a (1) _____ because you (2) _____ .
* Take water. You should drink (3) _____ per day.
* (4) _____ before you go, so you have the right training.
* Don't climb quickly. Go slowly to (5) _____ .

Irregular verbs

Infinitive	Simple past	Past participle
be /biː/	was / were /wɒz/, /wɜːr/	been /biːn/
be born /biː bɔːrn/	was / were born /wɒz/, /wɜːr bɔːrn/	been born /biːn bɔːrn/
become /bɪˈkʌm/	became /bɪˈkeɪm/	become /bɪˈkʌm/
begin /bɪˈgɪn/	began /bɪˈgæn/	begun /bɪˈgʌn/
break /breɪk/	broke /brəʊk/	broken /ˈbrəʊkən/
buy /baɪ/	bought /bɔːt/	bought /bɔːt/
choose /tʃuːz/	chose /tʃəʊz/	chosen /ˈtʃəʊzən/
come /kʌm/	came /keɪm/	come /kʌm/
do /duː/	did /dɪd/	done /dʌn/
drink /drɪŋk/	drank /dræŋk/	drunk /drʌŋk/
drive /draɪv/	drove /drəʊv/	driven /ˈdrɪvən/
eat /iːt/	ate /et/, /eɪt/	eaten /ˈiːtən/
fall /fɔːl/	fell /fel/	fallen /ˈfɔːlən/
feel /fiːl/	felt /felt/	felt /felt/
fight /faɪt/	fought /fɔːt/	fought /fɔːt/
get /get/	got /gɒt/	got /gɒt/
give /gɪv/	gave /geɪv/	given /ˈgɪvən/
go /gəʊ/	went /went/	gone /gɒn/
grow /grəʊ/	grew /gruː/	grown /grəʊn/
have /hæv/	had /hæd/	had /hæd/
hear /hɪər/	heard /hɜːrd/	heard /hɜːrd/
hit /hɪt/	hit /hɪt/	hit /hɪt/
know /nəʊ/	knew /njuː/	known /nəʊn/
learn /lɜːrn/	learnt / learned /lɜːrnt/, /lɜːrnd/	learnt / learned /lɜːrnt/, /lɜːrnd/
leave /liːv/	left /left/	left /left/
let /let/	let /let/	let /let/
lose /luːz/	lost /lɒst/	lost /lɒst/
make /meɪk/	made /meɪd/	made /meɪd/
meet /miːt/	met /met/	met /met/
put /pʊt/	put /pʊt/	put /pʊt/
read /riːd/	read /red/	read /red/
ride /raɪd/	rode /rəʊd/	ridden /ˈrɪdən/
run /rʌn/	ran /ræn/	run /rʌn/
say /seɪ/	said /sed/	said /sed/
see /siː/	saw /sɔː/	seen /siːn/
sell /sel/	sold /səʊld/	sold /səʊld/
send /send/	sent /sent/	sent /sent/
sing /sɪŋ/	sang /sæŋ/	sung /sʌŋ/
sit /sɪt/	sat /sæt/	sat /sæt/
sleep /sliːp/	slept /slept/	slept /slept/
spend /spend/	spent /spent/	spent /spent/
strike /straɪk/	struck /strʌk/	struck /strʌk/
swim /swɪm/	swam /swæm/	swum /swʌm/
take /teɪk/	took /tʊk/	taken /ˈteɪkən/
tell /tel/	told /təʊld/	told /təʊld/
think /θɪŋk/	thought /θɔːt/	thought /θɔːt/
wake /weɪk/	woke /wəʊk/	woken /ˈwəʊkən/
wear /weər/	wore /wɔːr/	worn /wɔːrn/
win /wɪn/	won /wʌn/	won /wʌn/
write /raɪt/	wrote /rəʊt/	written /ˈrɪtən/

Audio transcripts

IT'S MY LIFE

TRACK 02, P. 8

1	math	5	drama
2	art	6	music
3	history	7	science
4	ICT	8	geography

TRACK 03, P. 8

1 September sixteenth, nineteen ninety-six
2 February twenty-eighth, the year two thousand
3 May first, two thousand eleven
4 January third, two thousand fifteen

TRACK 04, P. 9

Chris: So, what's your name?
Lucy: My name's Lucy. What about you?
Chris: I'm Chris.
Lucy: Nice to meet you, Chris. What grade are you in?
Chris: I'm in 8th grade.
Lucy: Me too! I'm in Mr. Brown's class.
Chris: Cool. Where do you live?
Lucy: On Ash Road.
Chris: Oh, I live near there. Let's walk home together!
Lucy: OK, let's go!

UNIT 1
What do you like?

TRACK 05
(Text on p. 12)

TRACK 06
(Text on p. 17)

TRACK 07, P. 17

Judge 1: Hi, Zak.
Zak: Hi.
Judge 1: Well... you certainly have your own style of singing, which I like. but I think you need to work on your voice. It's not strong enough at the moment.
Judge 2: Yes, I agree with Donna. That's a beautiful song, but at the moment you aren't really expressing the feelings in it. Do you have singing lessons, Zak?
Zak: Er, no.
Judge 2: Well, you should have some. We're not saying you don't have talent. You do! But that's not enough on its own.
Judge 1: So this time, you aren't successful... but maybe in the next season you'll be one of the winners. Don't give up and good luck!
Zak: Er, thanks.
Judge 2: Well, Liz and Ben! That was a great performance! You move well and you look good together. Well done! Donna?
Judge 1: Mmm, I agree. How many hours a week do you practice, guys?
Liz: Two hours a day from Monday to Friday, and more on Saturdays and Sundays.
Judge 1: Well, it shows! Just one thing, though – try to relax more when you're dancing. You looked very serious, as if you weren't enjoying yourselves!
Ben: That's because we were nervous!
Judge 1: OK, fair enough. Anyway, congratulations! You go through to the next stage of the show!

TRACK 08, P. 20

Owen: Hi, Joe.

Joe: Hi, Owen. How's it going?
Owen: Fine. Listen, I've just seen something that sounds really interesting.
Joe: Oh yeah? What's that?
Owen: It's an ad for adventure weekends at an activity camp for teenagers this fall.
Joe: Ugh, sounds boring...
Owen: Why do you say that? You're into sport and stuff. It's just your kind of thing!
Joe: But doing group activities with people you don't like? Not me! We do that at school!
Owen: Oh, come on! How do you know you won't like the other people? Anyway, you don't get the chance to do things like this at school.
Joe: Yeah? So, what kind of things?
Owen: Sailing, photography, parkour...
Joe: Parkour? Can you do parkour at this place?
Owen: Yeah. And not only that – I'm looking at their website now and it says that one of the tutors is a famous parkour expert.
Joe: Oh wow! It's starting to sound interesting now. Listen, give me the website address, and I'll have a look at it.

TRACK 09, P. 21

Chris: Hello. I'd like to register for one of your adventure weekends.
Woman: OK, great! I just need a few details from you. What's your name?
Chris: Chris Bradley.
Woman: And what's your address, Chris?
Chris: It's 21 Ash Road.
Woman: OK. What's your cell phone number?
Chris: 766-8921.
Woman: OK. Do you have an email address?
Chris: Yes, it's chris@inmail.com
Woman: Can you spell that for me?
Chris: Yes. It's c-h-r-i-s at i-n-m-a-i-l dot com
Woman: Great, thanks. Oh, I nearly forgot! What's your birthdate?
Chris: April 4th, 2003.
Woman: OK, great. Here's a leaflet for you with more information about the camp.

TRACK 10
(Text on p. 23)

UNIT 2
Music and TV

TRACK 11
(Text on p. 25)

TRACK 12
(Text on p. 29)

TRACK 13, P. 29

Hazel: Hey James, how's it going?
James: Everything's fine, thanks. How are you?
Hazel: Great thanks! I'm just waiting for the bus...
James: Yeah, me too. Are you going home?
Hazel: No, I'm going to my friend's house.
James: Oh, right. I'm going home. It's my sister's birthday, so we're having a special meal.
Hazel: Yeah? Hey – did you watch *Life in the Wild* yesterday?
James: *Life in the Wild?* No, I didn't. What time was it on?

Hazel: About 5 o'clock, I think. On CBC.
James: No... What was it about?
Hazel: It was a documentary about penguins in the Antarctic.
James: Penguins? Was it any good?
Hazel: Yeah, it was amazing! Really interesting. It was about an expedition to study the penguins there. There were hundreds of penguins! It was so cold, but there were all these little baby penguins – they were so cute!
James: That sounds nice. Well, I watched a movie called *New Dawn.*
Hazel: *New Dawn?* What was that like?
James: It was terrible! The story was awful! It was really long and there were too many ads...
Hazel: Were there any famous actors in it?
James: No, I don't think so. I can't remember their names...
Hazel: Was it exciting?
James: No, it wasn't – not at all! And the special effects were terrible!
Hazel: Oh my. Anyway – here's my bus. See you tomorrow!
James: Yeah. See you later.
Hazel: Say Happy birthday to your sister from me!
James: I will. Bye!

TRACK 14, P. 32

Chloe: Hey, Lisa. How's it going?
Lisa: Hi there! I'm fine, thanks. What are you doing?
Chloe: I'm at the new youth club – you know, the one at the Community Center.
Lisa: Oh, yeah. Is it good?
Chloe: Yeah, it's nice. It's much better than staying at home! Anyway, what are you doing?
Lisa: Oh, I'm at home. I'm watching TV with Mom and Dad.
Chloe: Oh. You should come here next week!
Lisa: Yeah, maybe. Anyway, I'm calling to see if you want to play tennis tomorrow.
Chloe: Er, yeah, OK – if it doesn't rain! What time?
Lisa: Before lunch? How about 11 o'clock?
Chloe: Yeah, that's good. 11 o'clock at the park?
Lisa: Great!
Ben: Are you coming? It's starting soon.
Chloe: Yeah, I'm coming, just a minute.
Lisa: Who are you talking to?
Chloe: Oh, this boy called Ben.
Lisa: Ben? What's he like?
Chloe: Listen, let's talk tomorrow and I'll tell you all about it. The movie is starting now. It's Movie Night tonight.
Lisa: Oh! What are you watching?
Chloe: I'm sorry but I have to go now. See you tomorrow.

TRACK 15, P. 33

Ben: Let's think about the song playlist for the Party Night.
Chloe: Yes, great idea!
Ben: Do you like Will Robins?
Chloe: Yes, I love him!
Ben: What's your favorite song? How about *Players*?
Chloe: No, I prefer *Love.*

Ben: OK, that's fine. I like that, too.
Chloe: And what about Bankside?
Do you like them?
Ben: Oh, no. I can't stand them!
Chloe: Really? What else do you like, then?
Ben: I prefer Finn Woods. They're better than Bankside.
Chloe: OK. I don't mind Finn Woods. Which song do you like best?
Ben: I really like *Living there*. That's very popular.
Chloe: Great! And let's have something by Bright Things, too.
Ben: Yes. How about *Gems*?
Chloe: Perfect! OK. We have three songs so far!

TRACK 16
(Text on p. 35)

UNIT 3
Fact or fiction?

TRACK 17
(Text on p. 39)

TRACK 18
(Text on p. 43)

TRACK 19, P. 43
TV host: Tonight we're talking about important people in modern history and I'll be introducing tonight's guests in just a moment. First of all, we sent our reporter, Sam Jenkins, out and about to see what you had to say on the subject.
Sam Jenkins: Sorry to bother you – do you mind if I ask you something?
Woman: No, of course not.
Sam Jenkins: Which person in modern history do you admire the most?
Woman: Oh! That's a difficult question...
Sam Jenkins: We're doing a survey to find out what people think.
Woman: I see. Can it be anyone?
Sam Jenkins: Yes – a politician, a painter, an athlete... whoever. Someone that you think has made a difference to the world.
Woman: Well then, for me it's John Lennon. He was a talented singer and wrote some really beautiful songs. He believed that people should live in peace.
Sam Jenkins: OK, great! Thanks a lot for your time.
Woman: No problem.
Sam Jenkins: Hi there – do you have a minute? I just want to ask you a quick question.
Jason: Go ahead.
Sam Jenkins: We're trying to find out which famous person from modern history people admire. Who would you choose?
Jason: Well the only person I can think of is the guy who invented Facebook... what's his name?
Sam Jenkins: Mark Zuckerberg?
Jason: That's right. I'll choose him because I think Facebook was a really clever idea. I mean, it has completely changed the way people communicate.
Sam Jenkins: Right. Thanks! Er, and are you two together?
Woman 2: Yes.
Sam Jenkins: OK, so can I ask you the same question?
Woman 2: Yes, sure. I don't agree with Jason because I don't think Facebook is such an amazing invention.
Sam Jenkins: OK...

Woman 2: For me, this person has to be someone who really gives people hope. Like that teen girl, Malala Yousafzai. She defended girls' right to education in Pakistan and then a fundamentalist shot her. She almost died, but then moved to the United Kingdom with her family. She has won the Nobel Peace Prize, hasn't she? Well, I think she's amazing because her story shows that it's important to fight for our rights.
Reporter: Great. Thanks a lot! Well, we're going back to the studio now...

TRACK 20, P. 46
1
Your attention, please! The Scottish pipe band is starting soon on the Main Stage. That's the Scottish pipe band at 5 o'clock on the Main Stage.
2
Attention, everyone! This is an announcement about classes and activities. The African drumming class is starting now at the activity tent. All children welcome – under 16s only please for this event!
3
Your attention, please! Please make your way to the exits. The festival finishes in 30 minutes. Please make your way to the exits now. Thank you.

TRACK 21, P. 47
Hazel: Hi! Did you have a good weekend?
James: Yes, I did. It was amazing!
Hazel: What did you do?
James: I went to a music festival with my brother.
Hazel: Really? How was it?
James: It was fantastic! I saw some great bands.
Hazel: Wow! Cool.
James: Anyway, what about you? How was your weekend?
Hazel: Oh, it was all right.
James: What did you do?
Hazel: Nothing special. I went shopping.
James: Oh, well. Next time you can come with us!

TRACK 22
(Text on p. 49)

UNIT 4
Life on Earth

TRACK 23
(Text on p. 50)

TRACK 24
(Text on p. 55)

TRACK 25, P. 55
Chris: Which endangered animal are you going to do your project on?
Lucy: Whales, I think. I found this article about them on the internet and they're really amazing animals, you know.
Chris: What's so amazing about them?
Lucy: Well, first of all, they're really intelligent. For one thing, they have their own language.
Chris: What do you mean? Fish can't talk!
Lucy: They aren't fish! Honestly, Chris, don't you listen to anything in our biology classes? They're mammals!
Chris: OK, if you say so!
Lucy: Anyway, whales make sounds under the ocean in order to communicate with other whales.

Chris: Really? I didn't know that!
Lucy: Yes, and they're very friendly animals, too. When people go whale watching, the whales swim near the boats and look at the people!
Chris: Wow! I'd love to see a real whale.
Lucy: Me too. But soon there might not be any.
Chris: Why not? Whale hunting isn't allowed any more, is it?
Lucy: No, but they still do it in some countries. Another problem is ships.
Chris: Ships?
Lucy: Yes, sometimes ships hit whales and kill them by mistake.
Chris: That's terrible!
Lucy: I know. Anyway, what are you doing your project on?
Chris: Er, I haven't decided yet. Maybe snakes.
Lucy: Snakes? They aren't an endangered species, are they?
Chris: No, but I know a lot about them. My brother has a pet snake, you see.
Lucy: You're kidding! That's awful!

TRACK 26, P. 58
Conversation 1
Teen boy: The sand looks much cleaner now! Can we have a break? It's hot!
Teen girl: We can soon, but there's still plenty of trash to pick up!
Teen boy: Oh yeah, there are some cans over there ... Let's go and get them. Bring the trash bag over here!
Conversation 2
Teen girl: Here's our bus, John. That's it. One to Times Square, please.
Teen boy: And one ticket to Times Square for me too, please.
Bus driver: OK!
Teen girl: Thanks. Let's sit here.
Teen boy: What are we going to do now?
Teen girl: I'm going to take you to my favorite café. It has the best bagels in New York! Are you hungry?
Teen boy: Yes! And I love bagels!
Conversation 3
Mother: Right, Jake – here's the food for the giraffes. You can feed it to them by hand if you like.
Jake: OK. Like this?
Mother: Yes. Don't worry – they're very friendly. They're enjoying those carrots! Right, in a minute we're going to go over to the elephant house. The elephants like playing with water, so you might get a bit wet!
Jake: Yay! That sounds fun!
Mother: Yes, it is fun! Here, I have this waterproof jacket for you.
Jake: Great! Thanks, mom.

TRACK 27, P. 59
Coordinator: Hello there, how can I help?
Lucy: Hello, I'd like to sign up for the volunteer day.
Coordinator: Great! Do you want to help in the zoo gift store?
Lucy: That's a nice idea, but I want to help wildlife. I'd rather do something with the animals.
Coordinator: OK. How about cleaning the penguin pool?
Lucy: Well, I don't mind cleaning, but I don't really like water! Could I feed the animals?

135

Coordinator: Yes, maybe that's a better idea for you. You can help one of the zookeepers feed the elephants.

Lucy: Thanks! That sounds more interesting than the other activities.

Coordinator: No problem!

Lucy: Do you need any details from me?

Coordinator: Yes, could you please fill in this form?

Lucy: OK!

TRACK 28
(Text on p. 61)

UNIT 5
Special days

TRACK 29
(Text on p. 64)

TRACK 30
(Text on p. 69)

TRACK 31, P. 69
TV host: Now it's over to Rob Porter live in New York.

Rob: Thanks, Sophie! I'm here at Times Square, waiting for the Times Square New Year's eve ball to drop and the fireworks, of course! There are thousands of people here to celebrate the New Year. While we wait, I'm going to ask a few people if they've made any resolutions for the New Year. Hello! What are your resolutions for the new year?

Woman 1: I'm going to learn a new language – I want to learn Spanish!

Rob: Spanish? Great! And what about you?

Man 1: I'm going to exercise more regularly.

Rob: Great idea! How about you?

Woman 2: I'm going to eat well and be more healthy!

Rob: So many good intentions!

Teen boy: Yeah – I'm going to study hard and pass all my exams in the new year!

Rob: And how about you?

Woman 3: Me? I'm going to be happy and have more fun!

Rob: And that starts now, right? It's nearly midnight. Let's look at the ball...

TRACK 32, P. 72
1
Ann: Hi, I'm Ann. Next Wednesday, I'm going on a school trip to the Museum of Natural History. We're going to see an exhibition about space and the universe and all that...

2
Ben: Hello, this is Ben. Next weekend, I'm going on a trip to California to visit my relatives. We're all going to stay at my grandparents' house, and we're going to celebrate my grandma's 60th birthday with all the family.

3
Charlotte: I'm Charlotte and I'm going on a Scout trip to Wyoming. We're going to stay on a campsite right in the mountains – it's going to be amazing! We're going to climb the highest mountain in the state. I'm so excited!

4
David: Hello, I'm David. On Saturday, I'm going on a day trip with my best friend Peter and his parents. We're going to drive to a fantastic amusement park called Alton Towers. I'm going to go on the biggest rollercoaster! It's going to be fun!

TRACK 33, P. 73
Hazel: Hi there. What are you up to?

James: Oh, nothing special. I'm just going to class.

Hazel: Listen, are you free on Saturday?

James: Yes, I think so. Why?

Hazel: I'm going to the Harvest Festival, in Springfield. Do you want to come?

James: That sounds fun. Who else is going?

Hazel: My brother and my cousin Harry.

James: Great! What time are you going?

Hazel: We're leaving at 10 o'clock.

James: OK. Can I meet you at your house?

Hazel: Yes, sure. See you soon.

James: See you on Saturday!

TRACK 34
(Text on p. 75)

UNIT 6
Take care

TRACK 35, P. 76
a Exercise regularly
b Discuss your worries
c Don't get into arguments
d Take time for yourself
e Don't get stressed about exams
f Ask for help
g Don't worry about your appearance
h Try new sports
i Don't bully other people
j Eat a healthy diet

TRACK 36
(Text on p. 81)

TRACK 37, 81
Dr. Maggie: Hello. Teen helpline. This is Dr. Maggie. How can I help you?

David: Well, er, I have this problem and I don't know what to do about it.

Dr. Maggie: That's what I'm here for. Can you tell me your name?

David: David.

Dr. Maggie: OK, David. What's the problem?

David: I keep getting backache. I don't know why.

Dr. Maggie: Is your school bag very heavy?

David: Yes, it is quite heavy. And I ride my bike to school with my bag on my back.

Dr. Maggie: Do you carry it on both shoulders?

David: No, I don't. I carry it on one shoulder.

Dr. Maggie: Well, that's the problem, David. You're carrying all the weight of the bag on one side of your body, which is very bad for your back. Why is your bag so heavy?

David: I have to take a lot of books to school.

Dr. Maggie: Yes, but remember you don't need to carry all your books around with you all the time. Just take the books you need for that day.

David: OK, I will. Thank you for the advice.

Dr. Maggie: No problem, David. I hope you start feeling better soon.

Dr. Maggie: Hello. Teen helpline. This is Dr. Maggie. How can I help you?

Molly: Er, hello. My name's Molly. Can I ask your advice about something, please?

Dr. Maggie: Yes, of course, Molly. Go ahead.

Molly: Well, I've had lots of headaches recently and I'm not sleeping very well.

Dr. Maggie: Is anything else worrying you?

Molly: No, not really.

Dr. Maggie: How many hours a day do you spend on your computer?

Molly: About six – from three o'clock in the afternoon until nine o'clock every evening.

Dr. Maggie: I think that's too long, Molly. I'm not surprised you're getting headaches. Do you play any sports or get any exercise?

Molly: No, I don't. I hate sports! The only thing I love is playing computer games.

Dr. Maggie: Well, my advice to you is find another hobby. Don't stop playing computer games completely, but an hour a day is enough. If you start doing more exercise, I think you'll feel much better.

Molly: Do you think my headaches will stop?

Dr. Maggie: Yes, I do. I'm 99% sure the time you spend on your computer is the problem.

Molly: OK. Thank you.

Dr. Maggie: Thank you for your call. Bye, Molly.

TRACK 38, P. 84
Girl: What are you looking at?

Boy: I have this new "Travel Doctor" app for my phone. It's going to be great for the summer vacation.

Girl: Why? What does it do?

Boy: It has lots of information about first aid. Like if a bee stings you and you don't know what to do, it tells you. Look!

App: Bee stings. Here's what to do if a bee stings you.

Girl: Hmm... that happened to me once, actually.

Boy: And you can click here for a video showing you what you should do, step by step. This one shows you what to do if a snake bites you.

Girl: Oh, I bet that really hurts...

App: Snake bites. Here's what to do if a snake bites you.

Girl: Hmm, that's amazing! It's like having a doctor on your phone!

Boy: I know. There's advice for hundreds of different health problems. And it even tells you where the nearest drugstore is if you need to buy medicine or something.

Girl: Wow!

Boy: I'm going camping in Wyoming in August, so it'll be really useful if I have an accident or anything.

Girl: But just a minute – if you're camping on a mountain, miles away from anywhere, it's not really going to be very useful, is it?

Boy: Why not?

Girl: Because you won't be able to use your phone!

Boy: Oh, I didn't think of that!

TRACK 39, P. 85
Clerk: Hi there. What's the matter?

Nina: I have some mosquito bites on my legs.

Clerk: Oh! When did that happen?

Nina: They bit me yesterday when I was at the park.

Clerk: Oh, no! How do you feel?

Nina: I feel OK but they're really painful.

Clerk: Right. I think you should use this cream on the bites and make a doctor's appointment if they get worse.

Nina: Yes, I'll do that. How much is this?

Clerk: It's $3.99.

Nina: OK. Here you go.

Clerk: I hope you feel better soon!

Nina: Thanks!

TRACK 40
(Text on p. 87)

Learning bank

UNIT 1 What do you like?

I can contrast routines with actions happening now.

I always go swimming at the local sports center. This morning, I'm swimming in a different place. Do you go swimming in the mornings?

Free-time activities
- chat online
- do water sports
- go for a run
- go for a walk
- go shopping
- go to a café
- go to a theme park
- go to the gym
- hang out with your friends
- listen to music
- play computer games
- play volleyball
- send text messages
- surf the Internet
- watch a DVD

Simple present and present progressive
Grammar > p. 16

I can describe skills and abilities.

I can paint very well but I'm not very good at drawing. How about you?

Skills and abilities
- act
- climb walls
- cook
- dance
- draw
- drive a car
- jump
- paint
- play the drums
- ride a BMX bike
- sing
- speak English
- understand German

I can express likes and dislikes.

I love doing parkour, so I practice every day. I don't mind going out on cold days but I hate getting wet.

love, hate, (don't) like, don't mind, enjoy + -ing
Grammar > p. 19

UNIT 2 Music and TV

I can ask and answer about music, musicians, and bands.

A: *What's your favorite kind of music?*
B: *I really like pop music.*
A: *And what's your favorite band?*
B: *It's Maroon 5.*

Music

Kinds of music
- classical
- dance
- latin
- pop
- rap
- rhythm and blues (R&B)
- rock

Instruments
- bass
- drums
- guitar
- harmonica
- keyboard
- piano
- violin

Musicians
- backing vocals
- band
- choir
- composer
- conductor
- orchestra
- singer

I can describe and give my opinion on TV programs.

My favorite TV programs are comedies. I like them because they are funny.

TV programs
- cartoon
- comedy
- documentary
- drama
- game show
- movie
- music program
- reality show
- soap opera
- sports program
- talk show
- the news

Adjectives
- boring
- fantastic
- funny
- scary
- terrible

I can talk about past events.

When Catherine Hegarty started the Liverpool Signing Choir, it had 12 members. They became famous. They didn't invent a new kind of music; they invented a new way of singing. Last night's program wasn't very good. The actors were great but the guests weren't interesting.

Simple past – regular and irregular verbs (1): affirmative and negative / Be – simple past: affirmative and negative
Grammar > pp. 28 & 31

137

UNIT 3 Fact or fiction?

I can give my opinion on books.

A: *I'd like to read My Side because I like autobiographies.*
B: *I wouldn't like to read My Side. I think it's long and boring.*

Types of books

› adventure story
› autobiography
› biography
› comic novel
› cookbook
› detective novel
› fairy tale
› historical novel
› poetry book
› romantic novel
› science fiction novel
› thriller
› travel guide

Adjectives

› boring
› exciting
› fun
› funny
› interesting
› long
› useful

I can talk about famous people's lives.

John Lennon was a great musician.He was born in Liverpool, England. He wrote Imagine, which is a song about peace. A fan killed him in New York City.

Verbs to talk about people's lives in the past

Regular verbs

› created
› died
› earned
› killed
› opened
› produced
› wished

Irregular verbs

› began
› bought
› chose
› gave
› saw
› sold
› spent
› thought
› was born
› wrote

I can ask and answer about past events.

A: *Were you on vacation last week?*
B: *Yes, we were!*
A: *Where did you go?*
B: *We went to Europe. It was fantastic!*

Be – simple past: questions / Simple past – regular and irregular verbs (2): questions
Grammar › pp. 42 & 45

UNIT 4 Life on Earth

I can describe natural wonders and compare places.

I'd like to go to Mount Everest because it's amazing. It's higher than Aconcagua. It's the highest mountain in the world.

Geographical features

› beach
› canyon
› cave
› desert
› forest
› island
› lake
› mountain
› ocean
› rain forest
› reef
› river
› sea
› valley
› waterfalls

Adjectives

› amazing
› colourful
› dry
› high
› huge
› impressive
› interesting
› large
› salty
› unusual

Adjectives: comparative and superlative forms
Grammar › p. 54

I can talk about environmental issues.

Animals are losing their habitat because people are building new houses and roads.

Environmental issues

People...

› build new houses and roads
› cut down trees
› disturb animals
› hunt animals
› leave trash on beaches

Animals...

› die
› lose their habitat

Ice platforms...

› melt

I can ask and answer about quantity.

A: *Is there a hotel in the reserve?*
B: *Yes, there is.*
A: *Did you see any wildlife on the safari?*
B: *Yes, I did! I saw a lot of animals.*
A: *How many animals are there in the reserve?*
B: *There are a lot of animals — rhinos, elephants, leopards, crocodiles and giraffes but there aren't any lions or cheetahs!*

a / an, some, any, not much / many, a lot of, How much / many...?
Grammar › p. 57

UNIT 5 Special days

I can describe celebrations and special days.

A: *What do you do for Christmas?*
B: *We always decorate a Chistmas tree, send cards and give presents. Some people go to church.*

Celebrations
- decorate the house
- eat special food
- give presents
- go to church
- have a party
- have fun
- send cards
- sing songs
- visit relatives
- watch fireworks
- watch street parades
- wear a costume

I can talk about arrangements.

A: *What are you doing this Sunday?*
B: *I'm going to the Carnival of Blacks and Whites.*
A: *Are you doing anything special?*
B: *My friends are coming to my home and we're walking to town together in black clothes.*

Present continuous for arrangements
Grammar p. 71

I can express my intentions.

A: *When are you going to travel to New York?*
B: *I'm going to travel next Monday.*
A: *Are you going to post pictures of your trip?*
B: *Yes, I'm going to post a lot of pictures.*

Going to: affirmative, negative, and questions
Grammar p. 68

I can describe the way we do things.

I'm going to do my homework as quickly as possible.
I'm going to work hard and practice my English.

Adverbs of manner
- badly
- dangerously
- easily
- happily
- hard
- healthily
- loudly
- nicely
- quickly
- regularly
- well

UNIT 6 Take care

I can talk about physical and mental health, health problems, and first aid.

Physical and mental health
- ask for help
- bully other people
- discuss your worries
- eat a healthy diet
- exercise regularly
- get into arguments
- get stressed about tests
- take time for yourself
- try new sports
- worry about your appearance

Health problems
- a cold
- a headache
- a stomachache
- backache
- blisters
- feel sick
- mosquito bites
- sunburn

First aid
- adhesive bandages
- aspirins
- bandages
- insect repellent
- sunscreen

I can express purpose.

Pack a pair of shorts and T-shirts to be comfortable during the day. Bring sunscreen to protect your skin from the sun.

The infinitive of purpose
Grammar p. 83

I can ask for and give advice.

You shouldn't get into arguments. You should discuss your worries with your parents, a teacher, or a counselor.

Should: affirmative, negative, and questions
Grammar p. 80

On the Beat
2019 © Macmillan Education do Brasil

Published under Licence. First Published 2005, by Macmillan Publishers S.A.

Editorial manager: Patricia Muradas
Editorial supervision: Diego Rodrigues / Obá Editorial
Content creation coordinator: Cristina do Vale
Content editors: Ana Beatriz Moreira, Daniela Gonçala da Costa, Larissa Vannucci, Silene Cardoso
Content consultant: Viviane Kirmeliene
Art editor: Jean Aranha
Art assistant: Fabiana Martins
Art assistant: Denis Araujo
Art intern: Jacqueline Alves
Digital editor: Ana Paula Girardi
Editorial assistant: Roberta Somera
Editorial intern: Bruna Marques
Editorial coordination: Leonardo do Carmo and Patrícia Harumi / Obá Editorial
Proofreader: Alexandre Cleaver and Daniela Vilarinho / Obá Editorial
Design: Mayara Menezes do Moinho, Bruna Marchi, Carol Ohashi, Julia Anastacio and Patricia Ishihara / Obá Editorial
Photo research: Marcia Sato
Cover concept: Jean Aranha

Images: p.08: Macmillan Publishers Limited/Studio8, Olegganko/iStockphoto/Getty Images, MarySan/iStockphoto/Getty Images, filkusto/iStockphoto/Getty Images, lunifer/iStockphoto/Getty Images, Virtaa/iStockphoto/Getty Images, Niko1ay/iStockphoto/Getty Images, Sashatigar/iStockphoto/Getty Images. p.09: Macmillan Publishers Limited/Studio8. p.10: Macmillan Publishers Limited/Studio8. p.11: Macmillan Publishers Limited/Studio8. p.12: PIKSEL/iStockphoto/Getty Images, Cristian Lazzari/iStockphoto/Getty Images, DragonImages/iStockphoto/Getty Images, Adam Turner/iStockphoto/Getty Images, Aldo Murillo/iStockphoto/Getty Images, FlairImages/iStockphoto/Getty Images. p.14: Barrie Harwood Signs/Alamy/Latinstock, ZambeziShark/iStockphoto/Getty Images, Alan Wilson/Alamy/Latinstock, Adrelin Quarry, Mattjeacock/iStockphoto/Getty Images. p.17: Motionshooter/iStockphoto/Getty Images, Andyworks/iStockphoto/Getty Images, Loonger/iStockphoto/Getty Images, Clu/iStockphoto/Getty Images, Rich Legg/iStockphoto/Getty Images, Proxyminder/iStockphoto/Getty Images. p.18: Aleksle/iStockphoto/Getty Images, Sergiy Goruppa/iStockphoto/Getty Images. p.19: Christopher Futcher/iStockphoto/Getty Images. p.20: Dmitriy Shironosov/iStockphoto/Getty Images, RyersonClark/iStockphoto/Getty Images, Iurii Sokolov/iStockphoto/Getty Images, Migin/iStockphoto/Getty Images. p.21: Macmillan Publishers Limited/Studio8. p.22: Vincent Shane Hansen/iStockphoto/Getty Images. p.23: Katarzyna Bialasiewicz/iStockphoto/Getty Images, Eliza Snow/iStockphoto/Getty Images. p.24: WILKING/Reuters/Latinstock. p.24: Christopher Polk/Getty Images. p.25: dan4/iStockpjoto/Getty Images. p.26: David Munn/WireImage/Getty Images, Wong Pun Keung/Photoshot News/Latinstock. p.29: Nidwlw/iStockphoto/Getty Images, Jan Will/iStockphoto/Getty Images, Cristian Baitg/iStockphoto/Getty Images, CBS. p.30: Macmillan Publishers Limited, Jane_Kelly/iStockphoto/Getty Images, Urazovsky/iStockphoto/Getty Images. p.32: londoneye/iStockphoto/Getty Images, Art-siberia/iStockphoto/Getty Images, Mordolff/iStockphoto/Getty Images, Ljupco/iStockphoto/Getty Images, Rouzes/iStockphoto/Getty Images. p.33: Macmillan Publishers Limited/Studio8. p.34: 2010 Getty Images/iStockphoto/Getty Images. p. 35: Andrew Benge/Redferns/Getty Images. p.36: Jason_V/iStockphoto/Getty Images. p.37: Don Bayley/iStockphoto/Getty Images, Konstantin Tavrov/iStockphoto/Getty Images, Rolf_52/iStockphoto/Getty Images, Carl Joseph/Coleção privada. p.38: Kai Michaels, Lonely Planet, Bloomsbury Publishing Plc, Harper Collins, Penguin, Jehoshua Kilen. p.40: Linda Yolanda/iStockphoto/Getty Images, Juanmonino/iStockphoto/Getty Images, Blue_iq/iStockphoto/Getty Images, Alynst/iStockphoto/Getty Images, Pamela Moore/iStockphoto/Getty Images. p.43: 2010 Getty Images/iStockphoto/Getty Images, Marka/Alamy/Latinstock, Ruvanboshoff/iStockphoto/Getty Images, FLDphotos/iStockphoto/Getty Images, 2005 Getty Images/iStockphoto/Getty Images, Paul Bergen/Redferns/Getty Images, 2009 Getty Images/iStockphoto/Getty Images, General Photographic Agency/Getty Images, Gawrav Sinha/iStockphoto/Getty Images. p.45: Scholastic. p. 46: Alen Popov/iStockphoto/Getty Images, Jjwithers/iStockphoto/Getty Images, Ababsolutum/iStockphoto/Getty Images. p.47: Macmillan Publishers Limited/Studio8, Macmillan Publishers Limited. p.48: Juanmonino/iStockphoto/Getty Images, Icenando/iStockphoto/Getty Images. p.49: COLUMBIA PICTURES / Album/Latinstock. p.50: Ilona Budzbon/iStockphoto/Getty Images, Adventure Photo/iStockphoto/Getty Images, Maiteali/iStockphoto/Getty Images, Terraxplorer/iStockphoto/Getty Images, Johnny Lye/iStockphoto/Getty Images, kavram/iStockphoto/Getty Images, Stuart Black / robertharding. p.51: Ruslan Dashinsky/iStockphoto/Getty Images, Steve Krull/iStockphoto/Getty Images, Bartosz Hadyniak/iStockphoto/Getty Images, Gennadiy Poznyakov/iStockphoto/Getty Images, ultramarinfoto/iStockphoto/Getty Images. p.52: Travel Ink/Getty Images, Chrupka/iStockphoto/Getty Images. p.55: Sebatl/iStockphoto/Getty Images, Kksteven/iStockphoto/Getty Images, Josef Friedhuber/iStockphoto/Getty Images, KhunJompol/iStockphoto/Getty Images. p.56: brytta/iStockphoto/Getty Images, Anopdesignstock/iStockphoto/Getty, p.58: Frank Sebastian Hansen/iStockphoto/Getty, JoshSilverlock/iStockphoto/Getty Images, SandroSalomon/iStockphoto/Getty Images. p.59: Macmillan Publishers Limited/Studio8. p.60: javarman3/iStockphoto/Getty Images. p.61: apomares/iStockphoto/Getty Images, Steve Debenport/iStockphoto/Getty Images. p.62: FLDphotos/iStockphoto/Getty Images. p.63: Gianliguori/iStockphoto/Getty Images, Ericfoltz/iStockphoto/Getty Images, Sean Randall/iStockphoto/Getty Images, ingmar wesemann/iStockphoto/Getty Images, siete_vidas/iStockphoto/Getty Images, Therightthumb/iStockphoto/Getty Images, Andrey Danilovich/iStockphoto/Getty Images. p.66: Macmillan Publishers Limited/Studio8. p.64: AndDraw/iStockphoto/Getty Images, Stepan Popov/iStockphoto/Getty Images, Baona/iStockphoto/Getty Images, Gilaxia/iStockphoto/Getty Images. p.65: Lara Belova/iStockphoto/Getty Images, Tony Hopewell/Getty Images, ediaphotos/iStockphoto/Getty Images, Marilyn Haddrill/iStockphoto/Getty Images. p.66: Paul Moseley/Getty Images. p.70: Agencia Makro/LatinContent/Getty Images, Gary Tognoni/iStockphoto/Getty Images, Bart Kowski/iStockphoto/Getty Images. p.72: enviromantic/iStockphoto/Getty Images, Gannet77/iStockphoto/Getty Images. p.73: Macmillan Publishers Limited/Studio8. p.74: Lisa-Blue/iStockphoto/Getty Images, 400tmax/iStockphoto/Getty Images. p.75: michaeljung/iStockphoto/Getty Images, George Clerk/iStockphoto/Getty Images. p.76: littleny/iStockphoto/Getty Images, Dimitrios Stefanidis/iStockphoto/Getty Images, Fertnig/iStockphoto/Getty Images, Stephan Hoerold/iStockphoto/Getty Images, Juanmonino/iStockphoto/Getty Images. p.77: People Images/iStockphoto/Getty Images, People Images/iStockphoto/Getty Images, Yuri Arcurs/iStockphoto/Getty Images, Steve Debenport/iStockphoto/Getty Images, lisafx/iStockphoto/Getty Images, Thon Varirit/iStockphoto/Getty Images, Wichansumalee/iStockphoto/Getty Images. p.78: MachineHeadz/iStockphoto/Getty Images. p.81: NoDerog/iStockphoto/Getty Images, Grassetto/iStockphoto/Getty Images, Tatiana Popova/iStockphoto/Getty Images, Tatiana Popova/iStockphoto/Getty Images, lucato/iStockphoto/Getty Images, Savany/iStockphoto/Getty Images. p.82: Davor Lovincic/iStockphoto/Getty Images, Durva Rodrigues/iStockphoto/Getty Images, Macmillan Publishers Limited. p.85: Macmillan Publishers Limited/Studio8. p.86: omgimage/iStockphoto/Getty Images. p.87: Totajla/iStockphoto/Getty Images. p.88: PeopleImages/iStock/Getty Images. simonapilolla/iStock/Getty Images. Catherine Yeulet/iStockphoto/Getty Images. p.89: martin-dm/iStock/Getty Images. p.90: evgenyatamanenko /iStock/Getty Images. Marija Jovovic/iStock/Getty Images. p.91: Rawpixel/iStock/Getty Images. p.96: sturti/iStockphoto/Getty Images. p.97: Albert L. Ortega/Getty Images, Steve Debenport/iStockphoto/Getty Images. p.98: Frazer Harrison/Getty Images. p.99: Cristie Guevara/iStockphoto/Getty Images. p.100: Juan García Aunión/iStockphoto/Getty Images, tunart/iStockphoto/Getty Images. p.101: Joseph Okpako/WireImage/Getty Images, kristian sekulic/iStockphoto/Getty Images. p.103: ruvanboshoff/iStockphoto/Getty Images, Michael Putland/Getty Images, Rob Stothard/Getty Images. p.104: stocksnapper/iStockphoto/Getty Images, RobbieJack/Corbis/Getty Images. p.105: The LIFE Picture Collection/Getty Images, WILLSIE/iStockphoto/Getty Images, Chris Schmidt/iStockphoto/Getty Images. p.107: Marshall Bruce/iStockphoto/Getty Images. p.108: stockcam/iStockphoto/Getty Images. p.109: laflor/iStockphoto/Getty Images, photosbyash/iStockphoto/Getty Images, LazingBeeiStockphoto/Getty Images, John Carnemolla/iStockphoto/Getty Images, Nancy Nehring/iStockphoto/Getty Images. p.112: Holger Leue/iStockphoto/Getty Images, Nacho Calonge/Alamy/Latinstock, Heritage Film Project/iStockphoto/Getty Images, Kevin Dyer/iStockphoto/Getty Images, Cristianl/iStockphoto/Getty Images. p.113: MichaelDeLeon/iStockphoto/Getty Images. p.114: 1MoreCreative/iStockphoto/Getty Images. p.115: IvonneW/iStockphoto/Getty Images. p.116: /iStockphoto/Getty Images, Imre Cikajlo/iStockphoto/Getty Images, DC_Colombia/iStockphoto/Getty Images. p.117: energy/iStockphoto/Getty Images, g-stockstudio/iStockphoto/Getty Images. p.118: FINBARR O'REILLY/Reuters/Latinstock. p.119: Lintao Zhang/Getty Images. p.120: Viktor Glupov/iStockphoto/Getty Images, PeopleImages/iStockphoto/Getty Images, Vladimir Melnikov/iStockphoto/Getty Images. p.122: Christopher Bernard/iStockphoto/Getty Images, FooTToo/iStockphoto/Getty Images, Balazs Kovacs/iStockphoto/Getty Images. p.126: goodapp/iStockphoto/Getty Images, Choice graphx/iStockphoto/Getty Images, Christian Wheatley/iStockphoto/Getty Images, Javi Julio Sierra/iStockphoto/Getty Images, Joel James/iStockphoto/Getty Images.

All rights reserved.
Although we have tried to trace and contact copyright holders before publication, in some cases this has not been possible. If contacted we will be pleased to rectify any errors or omissions at the earliest opportunity.

MACMILLAN EDUCATION
Av. Brigadeiro Faria Lima, 1.309, 3º Andar – Jd. Paulistano
São Paulo – SP – 01452-002 www.macmillan.com.br
Call center: (11) 4613-2278
0800 16 88 77
Fax: (11) 4612-6098
Printed in Brazil

Dados Internacionais de Catalogação na Publicação (CIP)

M12n	McBeth, Catherine
1.ed.	On the Beat 2 / Catherine McBeth... [et al.]. – São Paulo: Macmillan Education do Brasil, 2019.
	ISBN: 978-85-511-0162-9 (aluno)
	ISBN: 978-85-511-0165-0 (professor)
	1.Língua inglesa. I. Crawford, Michele. II. Tiberio, Silvia Carolina. III. Martinez, Ron. IV. Título.
	CDD 420

Índice para catálogo sistemático:
1. Lingua inglesa
Bibliotecária responsável: Aline Graziele Benitez CRB-1/3129